P. 68

# Family
# Decision
# Making

# Family Decision Making
# An Ecosystem Approach

**BEATRICE PAOLUCCI**
Michigan State University

**OLIVE A. HALL**
El Camino College

**NANCY W. AXINN**
Michigan State University

BIP '86

**John Wiley & Sons**

New York / Santa Barbara / London / Sydney / Toronto

*Library of Congress Cataloging in Publication Data:*

Paolucci, Beatrice.
  Family decision making.

  Includes bibliographical references and index.
  1. Family life education.  I. Hall, Olive A., joint author.
II. Axinn, Nancy W., joint author.  III. Title.

HQ10.P35            301.42            76-39953
ISBN 0-471-65838-3

# Preface

This book is intended primarily for those students of the family who are concerned with learning how control over the events of everyday living is exercised. The focus is on the family organization whose task it is to make decisions and guide the actions of family members as they interact with their environments. The approach is ecological: attention is focused on the mutually sustaining transactions that couple people and environments as well as on the decisions the family organization makes to create harmonious adaptations so that the optimum development of humans is assured. The book has a future orientation. The authors do not call attention to the individual decisions families are currently making, such as which car to buy, how to educate their children, or how to balance the money flow, because such decisions may need attention today but may not be the critical family choices in the future. Instead, the book focuses on principles and concepts that may be as applicable and meaningful in ten years as they are today.

The book is intended for use in courses in home economics, human ecology, and the social sciences that view the family from an interdisciplinary stance. The book offers an alternative to separate introductory courses in family management and family relationships. It is not intended to be a comprehensive presentation of family management or family relationships and development concepts. Rather the intent is to offer a way of viewing the family ecosystem: the relationship of family members and environments. Family educators, counselors, and therapists should also find the book personally useful as well as a helpful resource for clients confronted with family problems or critical family decisions.

We wish to express our deep appreciation to our present and

former students and professional colleagues who have provided help-ful suggestions and examples that have enriched our discussions but who have above all honed our thinking and provided inspiration coupled with patience. We are especially indebted to Georgianne Baker, Arizona State University; M. Janice Hogan, University of Minnesota; and Beverly Anderson, Verna Hildebrand, Linda Nelson, and Jean Page of Michigan State University for their reviews and suggestions. We are especially grateful to the unidentified reviewers who raised significant questions, ideas, and encouragement. These valuable critiques aided us in bringing the project to closure.

Beatrice Paolucci
Olive A. Hall
Nancy W. Axinn

*East Lansing, Michigan*
*Los Angeles, California*
*June 1976*

# Contents

FIGURES xi

TABLES xii

INTRODUCTION 1

PART I: ELEMENTS OF THE FAMILY ECOSYSTEM 3

1. THE FAMILY'S FREEDOM TO CHOOSE 5
   Role of Decision Making in Families 6
   Images, Shoulds, and Reality 7
   Fate-Control Continuum 10
   Summary 13
   Selected References 14

2. COMPONENTS OF THE FAMILY ECOSYSTEM 15
   Fundamentals of the Family Ecosystem 15
   Elements of the Family Ecosystem 16
   *Organisms 18 · Environments 18 · Organization 19 · Family Boundaries and Interfaces 21*
   Open and Closed Families 22
   Controlled Family-Environment Exchanges 23
   Summary 25
   Selected References 26

3. THE FAMILY AND ITS ENVIRONMENTS 27
   Elements of the External Environment 27
   Environmental Factors Affecting Choice 30
   Influence of Natural Environment 34
   *Influences of technological environment 36 · Influences of regulatory systems 38*
   Alienation 49

vii

Summary 51
Selected References 51

4. FAMILY MEMBERS: PRIMARY INFLUENCERS
OF FAMILY DECISIONS 53
Perceptions 55
Perceptual Organization 56
Needs 58
Values 63
Sources of Values 64
Value Classifications 65
Moral Imperatives 67
Family Value Questions 68
Value Orientations 68
Summary 72
Selected References 72

5. FAMILY ORGANIZATION: DETERMINANT OF
FAMILY DECISIONS 74
Family Functions 75
Roles of Family Members 76
*Role Expectations 77 · Role conflict 77*
Family Forms 80
Family-Environment Costs and Benefits 86
*Self-Maintenance 87 · Substanance Producing
Activities 87 · Intergroup Interaction 88 ·
Creative Activities 88*
Summary 88
Selected References 89

PART II: PROCESSES OF ADAPTATION IN THE FAMILY 91

6. DECISION MAKING IN THE FAMILY ECOSYSTEM 93
Decision Making as Process 94
*Decision-Making Style 94 · Decision-Making Rule 95*
Habitual and New Responses 97
Types of Decisions 100
*Formal Properties 100 · Substantive Characteristics
100*
Interrelatedness of Family Decisions 105
*Central-Satellite Pattern 106 · Chain Pattern 108*
Family Decision Makers 109

Summary 110
Selected References 110

7. REDUCING UNCERTAINTY IN DECISION MAKING 113
   Intrinsic Motivation for Information Processing 114
   Information Processing 115
   *Information overload 116 · Information constraints 117 · Cognitive complexity 118*
   Information Accessibility, Cost, and Credibility 119
   *Accessibility 119 · Cost of information 120 · Information Credibility 120 · Risk and Uncertainty 121*
   Strategies for Choice 122
   *Pro and Con 123 · Maximum 124 · Minimax 125*
   Summary 126
   Selected References 127

8. MANAGING RESOURCES TO ACHIEVE GOALS 128
   Decision Making 129
   *Value clarifying 129 · Value-goal relationships 130 · Goal setting 131 · Standard setting 133 · Resource allocation 136 · Resource attributes 137 · Resource limitations 143 · Resource measures 143*
   Decision Implementing 144
   *Facilitating 144 · Checking 145 · Adjusting 145*
   Summary 146
   Selected References 147

9. COMMUNICATION AND THE MANAGEMENT OF CONFLICT 149
   Communication Within the Family 150
   *Dimensions of Communication 153 · Communication networks 154*
   Nature of Conflict 156
   *Power 158 · Coalition 160*
   Conflict Resolution 161
   *Assertiveness training 161 · Constructive aggression 162 · Negotiation 163 · "No-lose" method 166 · Conjoint family therapy 169*

Summary                                                      171
Selected References                                          171

10. EFFECTS OF FAMILY DECISIONS ON HUMANITY                  173
    Consumption                                              174
    Socialization                                            177
    Interdependence of Family (Private) and Societal
        (Public) Decisions                                   182
    Selected References                                      184

INDEX                                                        187

# Figures

1. Fate-Control Continuum   10
2. Interdependence of Components of Family Ecosystem   16
3. Relationship of Family Organisms to Environment   17
4. Interaction Between Man and His Near Environment   20
5. Interaction of Decision Maker(s) and Environment   23
6. Family As An Energy Driven Organization   25
7. Elements of the Ecosystem   28
8. Model For Viewing Alternatives in a Family Decision Situation   32
9. Decision Linkage   106
10. Adaptive Processes of the Family Organization   130
11. Exchangeability of Non-economic and Economic Resources   140
12. Guidance Principle: Relationship Between Guidance and Child's Need   143
13. Comparison of Standard with Level of Goal Attainment   146
14. Differences Between A "You-message" and an "I-message"   151
15. Communication Networks   154
16. Hypothetical Open and Closed Family Systems   155

# Tables

1. Variant Family Forms                                          81
2. Continuum of Decision Rationality                            101
3. Negotiation in Family Situations                             164
4. Summary Definition of Dimensions by Resource
     Categories                                                 180

# Introduction

Things need not just happen in a family; they can be decided. The responsibility and the burden of choice is a particular attribute of humanness. The quality of human life and the prospect of the family's continued survival within limited environmental settings depends, in large measure, on the decisions made in daily family living.

## AN ECOLOGICAL PERSPECTIVE FOR FAMILY DECISION MAKING

Much of family decision making is shaped by the environmental settings in which the family functions. These environments either constrain decision making or offer opportunities for the family. Because the physiological and psychological make up of family members differs, as do the environments in which they interact, it becomes essential to view decision making from an ecological perspective.

An ecological perspective is one of viewing organisms and environments in interaction. The focus is on the interaction; that is, how organisms affect environments they act upon, and how these environments affect organisms.

A family ecological perspective offers a holistic approach to the study of the family. It focuses on the family and those environments that directly affect it and over which it has some measure of control. Hence it examines not only relationships between family members (O—O relationships) or particular environments, such as the house and interiors (E—E relationships) but also the decisions and actions that occur as the family interacts with its many environments-natural and artificial. This perspective highlights the interdependence of

1

family members and environments. Because both the family and its environment change over time, the linkages between them must be continuously monitored, so that the effects of one on the other can be in some measure controlled. This day-to-day decision making is the major concern of families. Taken singly, these decisions may appear to make little impact. Viewed cumulatively, they can result in a major force shaping the quality of life possible for the particular family and affecting the destiny of humankind.

Understanding how families are linked to environments and what goes into decisions made by families can be useful in shaping the future of all families. What an individual family decides and does—its choice and action—makes a difference!

This book emphasizes the transactions of families and environments. The transacting process is one of deciding, acting, and reacting. Families perceive and interpret messages from their environment on the basis of past experiences and new information. They selectively decide what to do and behave accordingly.

It is the purpose of this book to stimulate the reader to continuously examine and better understand these transactional processes between family and environments. We examine how decisions made by the family transform the family unit as well as its environments. Analysis of family decision making should challenge the reader to rethink and redesign both decisions and the decision process.

The book is divided into two parts. Part I describes the rationale for viewing the family from an ecosystem perspective. It defines and discusses the elements of the family ecosystem: environments as the resource base for family functioning, family members as the primary influencers of decisions, and the family organization as the determinant of family decisions.

Part II examines the processes of harmonious adaptation of families and environments. How decisions are made in the family is examined. Emphasis is placed on information processing to reduce uncertainty. The management of resources and conflict are viewed as critical to change and adaptation. Finally, issues relevant to the future of human survival are examined from the perspective of the impact of family choices on the quality of life and family welfare.

# Part One
## Elements of the Family Ecosystem

# Chapter 1
## The Family's Freedom to Choose

The capacity to decide is a unique attribute of a human being. Decision making is a learned process rooted in the past, carried on in the present, shaping the future. This chapter discusses opportunities and responsibilities of families in making decisions that sustain and enhance the quality of life of family members and the vitality of the environments that surround them.

In its daily existence every family must make countless decisions. At times it has little experience or information on which to base decisions that can have far-reaching and unknown consequences. Responsibility for such decisions can seem frightening, almost overwhelming. Without conscious effort family members can slip easily into a passive role, letting fate make decisions. Family decisions, which are the focus of this book, involve a complex interplay between and among individuals and environments. In addition, family decisions reflect the interdependence of private and public choices. If the opportunity, responsibility, freedom, and burden of making decisions are freely accepted, individuals can build a foundation for healthy family membership and effective citizenship, for choice making is a basic human endeavor.

5

## ROLE OF DECISION MAKING IN FAMILIES

Wise decision making in families is crucial to creating home environments that will aid each person to develop his or her potential. The family of today has both the opportunity and responsibility to make decisions that will assure the continuance of all that makes people human—the ability to shape value systems, determine goals, and use resources judiciously in carrying out functions of loving, nurturing, caring, and educating. Appropriate decisions can improve the quality of life and preserve our natural environment.

The explosion of knowledge and the impact of technology has opened new opportunities and alternatives for the family. Environments have become more complex as humans have achieved both the opportunity to choose and the concomitant burden of making decisions. Tradition, fate, or past experience can no longer be used as primary determinants of family affairs.

Within the context of a rapidly changing environment, the dynamic family, through its central decision-making and decision-implementing activities, performs two functions: (1) it stabilizes and maintains the family's most important values, and (2) it brings about nondisruptive change. The family's task becomes that of making decisions that stabilize the family, thus giving it a sense of rootedness and, hence, security. Decisions made must also allow the family to adapt to rapidly changing environments and give each family member room for personal growth and development.

As it moves through its life-cycle the family makes critical decisions that allow it to accommodate change. External forces create new conditions of living, and correspondingly, the need for new and different ways of living in families. As family members grow, family interaction patterns must change, and the roles family members play within the family and in the community must be redefined. In addition to adjusting to continuous change, the family must cope with the varied pressures and tensions that change creates. Scientific and technological innovations and advances in mass communication have reduced differences and distances among people; they have also changed the family's perception of itself, stimulating changes in values and goals, and consequently, creating a need for new decisions.

Perhaps even more difficult than the new decisions forced by continuous and rapid change, is the making of those choices directed toward maintaining stability. Because families have a place and time in history and function in a given social setting, some changes are mandatory and imposed. But the uniqueness of a given family lies in the ways it decides to handle change. Families choose to retain and strengthen some values that are peculiar to their way of life. But, to maintain stability, these values must be viewed in relation to those of the external environment. The family must decide upon new ways to maintain values they hold in high priority and at the same time guide value changes over time.

Daily decisions about family members' internal and private affairs are crucial to the family. Also important are the choices they make as citizens when they exercise their voice and vote to influence public policy. The wisdom the family exercises in making both types of decisions affects not only the family's welfare but also affects all humanity. Clearly, the cumulative effect of everyday decisions made and implemented in the arena of the family gives meaning to life and shapes the world of today and tomorrow.

The rapidly changing world has made some family decisions more difficult, but it has made others easier. Because of the increased knowledge in the natural and behavioral sciences, families today can control more aspects of living than in earlier times; that is, less needs to be left to chance. For example, a young couple is considering whether to delay having a second child until both complete their college education. Both partners now work full time, share the care of their two-year-old child, and take one or two courses at the community college each term. Modern family planning methods enable the couple to decide to space their children and limit their family size. But at the same time new options and interdependencies demand more information and increased ability to make wise decisions. For example, although modern child-spacing methods are available the selection of an appropriate method for the particular persons involved requires specific and often highly technical information. The more serious the decision that is being considered, the more the family may want to rely on professional advice in making the choice.

## IMAGES, SHOULDS, AND REALITY

Decision making is based on the family's image of an ideal state, what it feels it should do, and what in reality it can and does do. If a family is to implement a decision, motivation for change must be present. Consider, for example, a young couple that has little money for housing or food because they cannot find employment. Both partners are conscious of the discrepancy between their present circumstances and what they consider to be necessary for meeting their basic needs.

Survival is a potent inducement for family members to make choices that bring them closer to their concept of a "good life." Dreikurs and Gray (1968, p. 10) point out that all living beings must function in ways compatible to some degree with their environment if they are to survive. What a family does is what it believes will ensure survival and status. The unusual patterns of behavior that sometimes develop within a family often reflect the kinds of responses family members are seeking from others and have learned to expect from them. Choice may be based, consciously or unconsciously, on what one expects to happen. As family members respond to one another's expectations, behavior is reinforced and tends to be repeated.

Of particular concern when family decisions are being made is the question of self-interest versus family welfare. Discrepancies may exist between individual desires and family interests. For example, a family may prefer that the mother spend her time caring for the family rather than seek paid employment outside the home. The mother may desire to work for pay and hire others to perform family tasks. From her perspective, the family's welfare as well as her individual desires are being met. A version of the economic man applies: "Man acting in his self-interest in economic affairs also acts in society's interest." (Lee, 1971, p. 2). The free enterprise system in theory is based on this idea; however, in reality, the economic system is much more complicated than this. The question of self-interests and group welfare is simply brought up here to indicate that they may not be the same; decisions acceptable to one member of the family may not be to the rest of the family. The family's conception of what "should" be might result in pressure being felt by the individual whose behavior does not conform to the group expectations.

A stressful situation often involves conflicts of values. For example, a high school graduate may decide to lie around on the beach all summer before entering college. His parents, who place high value on the work ethic, may pressure their son to look for a summer job, pay room and board during the summer, and help toward his college expenses. The anxiety produced by such value differences forces the family into a decision making situation that requires tension management. The family must analyze the tensions, how the present situation differs from the past when relationships were more pleasant, and how the present situation differs from what the family members desire.

Any kind of change is likely to force a family to make a decision, usually under conditions of risk or uncertainty. Change might occur suddenly and require major adaptations in life style (e.g., when a family's home is lost or severely damaged by flood or earthquake). Change may have been contemplated for a long time and yet be traumatic when it finally occurs (e.g., a widow moves to a retirement home). Change may be easier for some members of the family than it is for others, partly because of the external circumstances but also because some people can adjust to new conditions more readily than others can. As an illustration, consider the family where the father, the sole employed person, is transferred from one state to another. The father is not greatly affected by the move; he is kept busy with his work, and his associates can introduce him to his new community. The children feel the loss of former playmates, but when they start school they begin to make new friends. However, the wife, especially the mother of a preschool child, may find her circumstances far from what she desires. She has to initiate contacts with neighbors and community organizations to establish social linkage as well as find a family doctor, shopping centers and other marketplace facilities.

The roots of family images are grounded in what the family members consider to be desirable. What does the family aspire to do or be? Levels of aspiration can influence the kinds of decisions a family wishes to make as well as the outcomes of decisions made. When essential human needs are satisfied, families can aspire to grow and develop in creative areas. Their decisions no longer have to center around survival needs but can be concerned with helping each family member develop his or her potential. The potentialities of what *can be* depend in part on the conceptions the family has of what *should be.* Families who expend most of their energy to survive and maintain their status probably have very restricted ideas of what *could be.* Part of the challenge of studying choice making in the family is to expand awareness of the many options open to families.

The degree of discrepancy between the reality of a family's present situation and the family's conception of what should be must fall within an optimal range. If very little discrepancy exists, the family is not likely to exert much effort toward change. On the other hand, if the discrepancy is extreme, the family might be unable to face the problem. Just as individuals flee from problems that seem overwhelming, families may deny that a problem exists, attempt to run away from it, or fight anyone or anything that is in their way. An optimal amount of discrepancy is large enough to motivate the family to work toward the desired condition yet small enough to make it seem possible for a decision or series of decisions to be made that could fulfill at least some of the family's goals. This philosophy determines the conversion of "images" into "shoulds" and creates a predisposition to decide.

## FATE-CONTROL CONTINUUM

In reality, how much freedom of choice does a family have? Freedom might be defined as the ability a family has to do what it wants to do. Having an image of a desired state and noticing that this image differs from present reality is the beginning of a decision situation. What determines a family's image of what could be? Tunnel vision causes people to close off many possibilities and limit their options needlessly. Certain environments offer very limited options (e.g., families where money is extremely limited, countries where food is in short supply, and homes which are so overprotective that a child is seldom permitted outside the house). Nevertheless, most families probably have much more freedom to create images and make decisions than they ever use.

Many philosophers have long debated the question of how much freedom of choice humans actually have. Opinions range from an assumption of minimum or no freedom (fate) to complete freedom (man in complete control). Levy (1963, p. 68) has conceptualized humanity's jurisdiction over its decisions on a continuum that ranges from complete absence of control to total control (see Figure 1).

At one extreme on the fate-control continuum, people are view-

| Fate | Fate exclusive of moral choice | Ego-based determinism | Culturally based determinism | Control |
|------|------|------|------|------|

Figure 1. Fate-Control Continuum

ed as puppets manipulated by unseen strings held by an invisible source. Life patterns are predetermined and maintained by a supernatural authority. Self-determination and decision making are viewed as myths.

The second point on the continuum, fate exclusive of moral choice, limits options to moral choices—all else is viewed as predetermined. One is allowed choices within a clearly defined moral code. At the third point on the continuum, ego-based determinism, choice is limited by one's own heredity and developmental experience. Culturally based determinism suggests that mores, folkways, and social codes and pressures determine choice (Hoyt, 1969, pp. 16–26, 66–75).

Those people at the farthest end of the fate-control continuum see themselves in control of the world. They believe that humans can control any situation, that they can find a way to conquer any obstacle; i.e. that where there is free will there is a way. Is it possible for a human being to really be in command of life, the immediate environment, and even of the larger world in which one resides? Is the omnipotent self merely an illusion?

Somewhere along this continuum is a range within which true freedom is likely to be found. The degree of freedom enjoyed varies from one person or family to another and from one situation to another. True freedom requires acceptance of responsibilities as well as a degree of maturity. A four-year-old child needs a parent; the child is not mature enough to make all decisions. When an individual is free to choose, unwise and unsound decisions as well as sound decisions may occur. The mature decision maker recognizes this possibility, tries to minimize the number of poor decisions made, and accepts responsibility when the outcomes of decisions are disappointing.

The idea of responsibility goes still further. Responsible individuals recognize limits to freedom; they are concerned about how their behavior will affect the well-being of family and society. To a considerable extent we are free to choose what we will be involved with and how responsible we will be for our environment. A person who contributes four hours a week as a volunteer at the local hospital has made a decision that benefits the community. How free was the choice? If one feels pressured, by other people or other groups, one may act in a certain way not because it is what one wishes to do but rather because it is what that person feels "ought" to be done.

Decisions are influenced not only by the present situation but also by past decisions. Decisions have a sequential effect; a decision made in the present may be influenced by past decisions and may influence future decisions and actions. Past decisions can place bounds on current options and can sometimes result in severe limitations. For example, a child who decides to climb a deserted mountain late in the day might slip and become crippled for life, or a family might suffer severe financial constraints as a result of over-commitment to installment purchases.

Accepting the idea that past decisions limit present choices helps one to see the significance of present decisions for the future. Decision making can also impose a pattern on the future. Families need not just drift along, merely responding to life's demands. Rather, the "free family" can make choices based on a consideration of what they want and a recognition of the consequences of the decision for others and for the future of society.

Vickers (1965, p. 13) urges that family members view themselves "not as a holder of a particular role but as a controller of an individual life, managing through the years a bundle of interlocking and partly inconsistent roles." Family roles can limit awareness and action. In some cases, behaving as a student, a family member, or an employee has constrained a choice. How free are individuals to act independently rather than as a member of a group playing a particular role?

Family settings range from those that are highly restricted to those in which nearly complete freedom exists. How much freedom can a family handle? When families are presented with too many options they become immobilized; they become "stimulus bound." Some families suffer from "option glut." There appear to be too many options. Others have too few options and relatively no choices open to them.

Kaufmann (1973, pp. 4—31) declares that many people suffer from decidophobia, the fear of making decisions. Their fear of autonomy causes them to crave a life without choice. Some of the strategies he suggests that people may use to avoid decisions or bias alternatives so choice will be clearly right include:

*Drifting* enables one to leave things to chance or go along with the *status quo.*

*Pedantry* keeps a person so absorbed in microscopic distinctions that he or she never gets around to major decisions, perhaps is never even aware of macroscopic alternatives.

*Allegiance to a school of thought, movement or religion* that provides a sense of belonging and overcomes the dread of standing alone; as a member of an organization, one is shielded from facing isolated, fateful decisions.

*Exegetical thinking* enables a person to read his own ideas into a text and get them back endowed with authority. This approach provides a prop; one never has to stand up and say what one thinks.

*Manichaeism* insists on the need for a decision but the choice is loaded so the decision practically makes itself. In this view there is a tendency to see only good on one side and only evil on the other.

*Marriage* can be used as a strategy for leaving fateful decisions to the spouse or for acting as a committee of two—presuming consensus when none really exists, denying responsibility if something turns out badly because each partner merely went along with the other.*

In contrast to these combinations of the decidophobic, Kaufmann asserts that an autonomous person chooses with open eyes, accepts the possibility of error, and has the courage to stand by his or her own beliefs.

## SUMMARY

The total family group, acting in support of the individual member, can provide security for autonomy. Life is autonomy in action, it provides freedom to choose coupled with responsibilities. The family is a basic setting for exercising this autonomy. The options the family exercises in shaping everyday activities can result in the most disquieting of human actions and emotions or the opportunity for the most reassuring of human experiences.

*From *Without Guilt and Justice: From Decidophobia to Autonomy* by Walter Kaufmann. Copyright 1973 by Peter H. Wyden, Inc.

## SELECTED REFERENCES

Dreikurs, Rudolf, and Loren Gray. *Logical Consequences.* New York: Meredith Press, 1968.

Hoyt, Elizabeth E. *Choice and the Destiny of Nations.* New York: Philosophical Library, 1969, pp. 16-26, 66-75.

Kaufmann, Walter. *Without Guilt and Justice: From Decidophobia to Autonomy.* New York: Peter H. Wyden, 1973.

Lee, Wayne. *Decision Theory and Human Behavior.* New York: John Wiley & Sons, 1971.

Levy, Charles S. "Decision Making and Self-Determination." *Adult Leadership.* 12, 3 (September 1963): pp. 68-69.

Vickers, Sir Geoffrey. *The Art of Judgment.* New York: Basic Books, 1965.

# Chapter 2
# Components of the Family Ecosystem

How family members interact with one another is shaped not only by the personalities that comprise the family unit but also by the complex set of environments that surround and sustain them. This chapter views the family as an ecosystem whose dynamic organization seeks to adapt family members and environments to one another so that they are mutually supportive.

## FUNDAMENTALS OF THE FAMILY ECOSYSTEM

Family members, their external environments as perceived by them, and the web of human transactions carried out through the family organization constitute the basic elements of the family ecosystem. This view of the ecosystem is consistent with formulations of general ecology (Odum, 1971, pp. 3-6). One fundamental characteristic of the family ecosystem is that it is made up of a collectivity of interdependent but independent parts working together to achieve a common purpose. Each element (organism and environment) is interrelated. Each element affects the other: organisms are related to organisms, environments are related to environments, and organisms are related to environments. Figure 2 focuses on the specific

15

$E \longrightarrow O$     Environment affecting family organisms (members)

$O \longrightarrow E$     Family organisms affecting environment

$O \longrightarrow O$     Family organism affecting family organism

$E \longrightarrow E$     Environment affecting environment

$O \longleftrightarrow E$     Reciprocal affect of family members and environments

Figure 2. Interdependence of Components of Family Ecosystem

relationships of family members to environments. Family members relate to one another through a web of information patterns. For example, parents exchange information with children, children change their behavior, and parents respond with changed behavior. Environments interact with one another, as when energy from the natural environment in the form of plants is transformed into food by the technological environment. and when the technological environment redefines the natural environment by emitting pollutants as well as by providing food for consumption. Organisms interact with environments when energy from the natural and human-built environments in the form of food is transformed by the family organization into meals. These meals provide both physiological and social nurturance for family members, and through them the family organization returns to the environment both productive people (labor) and wastes. These continuous exchanges and transactions between elements result in change and adaptation for all parts of the family ecosystem. The family organization can change or alter its internal relationships and functioning or it can alter the environment.

## ELEMENTS OF THE FAMILY ECOSYSTEM

The basic elements of the family ecosystem are: (1) organisms (family members) (2) environments (natural and human-built) and (3) the family organization, which functions to transform energy in the form of information into family decisions and actions (see Figure 3). An ecosystem approach to viewing family decisions forces one to look both at the persons involved in the decision process and the conditions that surround them. This ecological approach involves "a search for understanding and controlling the mutually sustaining

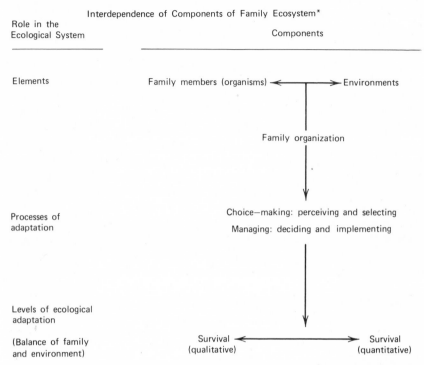

Figure 3. Relationship of family organisms to Environment (Adapted from *Population, Environment, and Social Organization: Current Issues in Human Ecology* by Michael Micklin. Copyright © 1973 by The Dryden Press. Reprinted by permission of Holt, Rinehart and Winston.)

relationships that couple men with his environment. . . . " (Hook and Paolucci, 1970, p. 316). Understanding the potentially far-reaching consequences of transactions between family members and environments provides information for decision making, decision implementing, and assistance in predicting decision consequences. Controlling implies that informed decisions will be made and that the family will develop strategies to insure that these conscious decisions are carried out.

The ecological system framework highlights the *interdependence* of organisms and environments. It focuses on those decision points where family members and environments interact and interrelate. The family organization mediates the relationships between family members and environments.

## Organisms

Family members, viewed as a set of interacting, interdependent but independent persons working together are defined in an ecosystem framework as organisms. This set of people, the family, function within a limited territorial domain. The character of the family is significantly different from that of its individual members. The family is viewed as a set of mutually interdependent organisms; intimate, transacting, and interrelated persons who share some common goals, resources, and a commitment to one another that extends over time. It is a corporate unit having symbiotic relationships. Its unit character, that is, its value system and cyclic development, differs from the characteristics of the individual members. Its territory is usually circumscribed within a house, neighborhood, or community.

## Environments

Broadly defined, the environment includes anything external to the family that can affect it. Life is maintained by drawing upon the resources of the environment, and the central task of the family organization is to decide how resources will be used by family members. Through continuing dynamic choice and management processes, the family acts upon the near environment, and the near environment acts on the family.

The environments that impinge on the family can be classified in a variety of ways. At the basic level the family is absolutely dependent on the natural environment, the source of energy, information, and matter. In particular, humans depend on the natural environment for water, air, food, each basic to survival.

Over time humans have, through the use of technology, altered the natural environment so that it has become more "human-built." Systems of agriculture and industry in particular have transformed the natural environment so that people could use that environment in diverse ways. In addition, humans have evolved sociocultural symbols and institutions that facilitate the family's ability to cope with the changing natural environment. These environments provide the information (norms, values, rules) for making decisions as well as the transformed energy (resources such as materials and dollars) for family activities.

There are three components of the environment: biophysical,

psychosocial, and technological. The biophysical environment of sun, land, water, air, space, plants, and animals interacts with the physiological and metabolic processes of the human system and makes it possible for the human to live. The psychosocial component, which includes the kinship, religious, political, economic, productive, recreative, symbolic, and ideological aspects of the near social environment, provides the data for shaping the interpersonal relations of the individual and family behavior patterns. The technological component, that is, materials, tools, and techniques of the physical and social environment, is used by families to manufacture objects or in some way alter both people and environments.

## Organization

The family organization, processing information from its environments, coordinates the activities of family members for the achievement of some common goal by dividing the tasks among family members and delegating the authority and responsibility for seeing that these tasks are carried out and family purposes achieved. The family organization is the processing system that transforms matter-energy and information and directs it toward family goal achievement. The environment is the source of family resources vital to family survival. The family organization transforms these resources into useful forms for family consumption. The family organizes itself, through choice making and managing processes, to transform energy into useful, life-supporting, and life-enhancing forms: consumption of food, clothing, shelter, for mere physical survival; socialization, aesthetic and educative activities to enhance the human potential of its members. By the way families choose to sustain and socialize members, they help define the environment, and, in turn, the environment enhances or limits the potentials for human development. Families, through judicious organization, can help maintain their environments and enhance the quality of life for their members as well as satisfy human aspirations.

The transactions between family members and their environments occur through the transformation of energy in the form of information and material and nutrient flows. This information stimulates the interchanges between family members and their environments. Compton and Hall (1972, p. 5) have identified some of these stimuli and the human responses they evoke (see Figure 4).

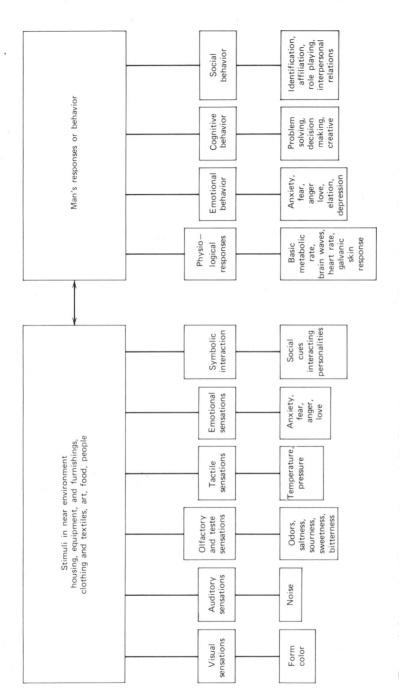

**Figure 4.** Interaction Between Man and His Near Environment (From *Foundations of Home Economics Research: A Human Ecological Approach* by Norma Compton and Olive Hall. Burgess Publishing Company, 1972.)

## Family Boundaries and Interfaces

When studying the family ecosystem, it must be kept in mind that family boundaries are not static, they are flexible. Boundaries are determined by the influx of information to the family from the particular environment or environments with which it is interfacing.

The interface is that point at which families and environments meet. It is here that information is exchanged and relationships are determined. New opportunities and problems emerge at these points. This results in the adaptation of one system to another (Auerswald, 1971, p. 278). Kantor and Lehr (1975, p. 24) describe interactions between a family and a particular environment:

> As the Orange family moves into its new neighborhood, it encounters a complex set of ongoing social conditions and institutional arrangements. At the interface of their family-unit subsystem with the outside world, family members become aware of how the new neighborhood differs from their previous one. The location of such institutions as library, gymnasium, school, and town center are discovered and mapped out for future reference. So, too, are people in the neighborhood. Conversely, those already living in the community begin to assess the newcomers . . . . Both neighbors and the new family cue each other, signaling certain persons to come closer and informing others to remain at a distance. Before long, the relations between the family and its new community begin to crystallize. Family members become receptive to certain elements in their new culture and unreceptive to others. Likewise, various members of the community are attracted to different family members for different reasons.*

The conditions that exist at the interface determine the kind of transformations that will occur. If transactions support both the family and the environment, new alternatives and opportunities emerge. If the transactions are not supportive, problems occur.

*From *Inside the Family* by David Kantor and William Lehr. Jossey-Bass Publishers, 1975.

## OPEN AND CLOSED FAMILIES

The family is a semi-open system. That is, it is open to interchanges with its various environments yet at times closed to new information. In fact, interchange between the family and environments is essential to the family's survival. Families differ in their degree of openness. Family members who interact primarily within the family system—those who are "turned inward"—tend to be isolated from their environments. Because they close out information from the environment, their alternatives are limited, and they find it difficult to adapt to change. Family members who interact with many environments—those who are "turned outward"—tend to be open. They are receptive to information from the environment, and, for them, opportunities and alternatives abound. There is opportunity for considerable flexibility and adaptation to change.

To survive families need to maintain a measure of both "openness" and "closedness"; they must be both flexible and stable. Families differ in their ability to adjust to changed situations and how much change they can accommodate before reaching the point of collapse. The more complex an ecosystem, the more successfully it can survive and resist stress. The more alternatives available to a family, the greater freedom that family has to establish satisfactory alternative pathways to optimum development. A complex network, with crisscrossed interconnections, enables the family structure to resist collapse through flexibility. Concurrently, the family can attain a degree of stability.

Some simple, static, relatively direct connections can provide a measure of stability at given points in time. The family ecosystem are subject to both centrifugal and centripetal forces. The centrifugal forces pull family members together into a rooted and tightly connected, semi-closed unit of intimacy and love. The centripetal forces open and connect the family to everwidening environments, to new options and alternatives. Thus the family has both rootedness and connectedness. It acquires both stable and flexible characteristics. There must be suffcent stability so that the system maintains itself, yet enough flexibility to allow for development and adaptation.

## CONTROLLED FAMILY-ENVIRONMENT EXCHANGES

Family ecosystems are dynamic, purposive organizations. They have preferred states, outcomes, and goals. The interchanges within the family ecosystem are cybernetic, that is, controlled. This controlled system depends on feedback, the process by which the family organization informs its members about how to relate to one another and

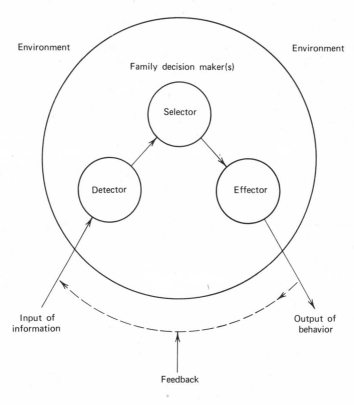

**Figure 5.** Interaction of Decision Maker(s) and Environment (Adapted from *Unified Social Science* by A. Kuhn. Dorsey Press, 1975).

to its environments in order to carry out activities. A controlled system knows and is able to narrow the gap between what is and what ought to be and reflects this in its goals (Kuhn, 1974, pp. 25-26).

The decision makers within the family organization monitor and direct the information flows and interactions between the family and environments. They control the relationships so that family goals can be achieved. In order to respond differently to different circumstances the family decision makers must be able to (1) detect the state of the environment by perceiving, receiving, and identifying environmental stimuli, (2) select one response rather than another, and (3) carry out the selected responses that will implement or affect the family's behavior or that of an individual member (Kuhn, 1975, pp. 35-38; see Figure 5).

The selected actions affect the environment, either changing it so that it better serves the needs of the family members or changing the relationships among family members in order to adapt to the environment. This interchange between family organisms and environments is the informational feedback controlled by the family organization. The feedback mechanism is basic to the family's adaptive function, it amplifies and intensifies flows of information. Feedback both stabilizes and changes the family ecosystem. This continuous oscillation between change and constancy keeps the family ecosystem in equilibrium, yet because the system does not return to the same point, it is always developing and evolving. Through the feedback process the family organization becomes self-regulating, self-directing, and self-organizing. That is, it can take corrective action to maintain equilibrium or stability, or it can disrupt a given state of equilibrium and bring about change. These processes of corrective action are referred to as *morphostasis* and *morphogenesis*. Morphostasis "refers to those processes in complex system-environment exchanges that tend to preserve or maintain a system's given form, organization, or state. Morphogenesis (refers) to those processes which tend to elaborate or change a system's given form, structure, or state" (Buckley, 1967, p. 58).

Families perceive and respond to their environments differently under different conditions and at different times, hence different conditions can lead to similar ends and similar conditions can lead to different outcomes. Buckley (1967, p. 79) defines these processes of coping with changing stimuli and maintaining balance as *equifinality*

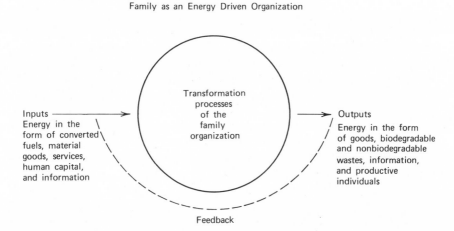

Figure 6. Family As An Energy Driven Organization

(different initial conditions resulting in similar ends) and *multifinality* (similar initial conditions leading to different ends). Understanding these concepts of the family ecosystem can be useful in developing alternatives for decision making.

The family is an energy-driven orgainzation (see Figure 6). The family ecosystem is *open* to *inputs* of *matter-energy and information* from the environment. It processes, transforms, and controls these inputs and directs them toward certain goals, which *feed back* into the environment thus adapting the elements of the ecosystem to one another and toward a balance or *equilibrium* (Paolucci and Hogan, 1973, p. 12).

## SUMMARY

A family ecology perspective, which focuses attention on family members *and* their environments allows one to better understand problems and arrive at solutions because it forces one to look at each part of the ecosystem and the relationships among them. Thus, families can learn to be efficient stewards, not just manipulators, of their environments, understanding that a reverence for life is dependent upon a concomitant reverence for its conditions.

## SELECTED REFERENCES

Auerswald, Edgar H. "Families, Change and the Ecological Perspective." *Family Process.* 10, 3 (September 1971): 263-280.

Buckley, Walter. *Sociology and Modern Systems Theory.* Englewood Cliffs, N.J.: Prentice-Hall, 1967, p. 59.

Compton, Norma, and Olive Hall *Foundations of Home Economics Research: A Human Ecological Approach.* Minneapolis, Minn.: Burgess Publishing, 1972, p. 5.

Hook, Nancy C., and Beatrice Paolucci. "The Family as an Ecosystem." *Journal of Home Economics.* 62, 5 (May 1970): 315-318.

Kantor, David, and William Lehr. *Inside the Family.* San Francisco: Jossey-Bass Publishers, 1975.

Kuhn, Alfred. *The Logic of Social Systems.* San Francisco: Jossey-Bass Publishers, 1974, pp. 20-59.

Kuhn, Alfred. *Unified Social Science.* Homewood, Ill.: Dorsey Press, 1975, pp. 35-38.

Micklin, Michael. *Population, Environment, and Social Organization: Current Issues in Human Ecology.* Hinsdale, Ill.: The Dryden Press, 1973, p. 7.

Odum, Eugene P. *Fundamentals of Ecology.* 3rd ed. Philadelphia; W. B. Saunders, 1971, pp. 3-6.

Paolucci, Beatrice, and M. Janice Hogan. "The Energy Crisis and the Family" *Journal of Home Economics.* 65 (December 1973): 12-15.

# Chapter 3
# The Family and Its Environments

Environments contain the resources essential to life functions. The natural environment is the source of all energy, which, when transformed, provides the means for human activity. The immutable rules of nature and the ever-changing rules designed by humans guide the adaptation of people and environments to one another. The bases for these rules are examined through viewing the family and its environments.

## ELEMENTS OF THE EXTERNAL ENVIRONMENT

The human-built and natural environments that interact with family members in large measure influence the kinds of decisions families make. What family members do and have is subject to environmental constraints. The family is generally viewed as a semi-open system. Inputs from the environment enter into the family and help shape its decision outcomes. In turn, families help shape environments by the decisions they make. Understanding how the family is linked to its environment provides an information base for making decisions that will help insure humanity's continuance. People determine the rules and guides for making decisions in the technical and social environ-

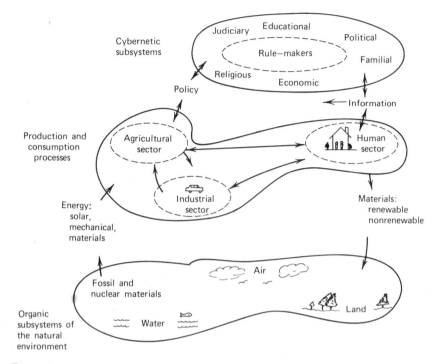

**Figure 7.** Adapted from Koenig–Edens conceptual diagram, p. 107. Elements of the Ecosystem.

ments. In the natural environment of land, water, and air, rules are inherent, but too often ignored by man.

Koenig et al. (1975) have identified three environmental systems that help shape family options: the natural system, technological, agricultural-industrial system, and social regulatory system. The natural system is comprised of the structure of the landscape without the presence of humans. The manufactured agricultural-industrial complex is superimposed on the natural landscape and, through technology, transforms matter-energy into food, fiber and material goods. The social regulatory systems are structures created by people to maintain integrity between the human sphere and the natural environment (see Figure 7).

The family is a basic producing, socializing, and consuming system that is inextricably linked to its external environments through material and energy flows (Paolucci and Hogan, 1973, p. 12). It is related to other social groups through the sharing of access to particular energy sources (electric power, coal, gas) and by participation in a web of nutrient and information flows.

In the natural environment, structured materials comprise the entire ecological system, which in the final analysis is driven by a continuous flow of energy from the solar system. From these structured chemicals and materials, biological communities have evolved to form closed material cycles. Each lake, stream, and watershed has a limited capacity to process materials of given types in order to maintain "balance." This is a given rule or principle of the natural environment.

A characteristic of any system is that everything must go somewhere. Nature has a remarkable capacity for recycling "wastes" and releasing them to other parts of the environment as nourishment. Human beings are beginning to learn that nothing simply goes away; it is transferred from one place to another and converted from one form to another. Families can unwittingly make decisions that defy this principle when they discharge toxic wastes into the natural environment or when they inject nonbiodegradable materials into the natural environment.

The natural environment is humanity's life support system for it provides those resources that sustain life—materials and energy. Through the artificial transformation systems of agriculture and industry, families are provided innumerable options of food, clothing, shelter, and transportation. For prudent decision making, families must understand that everything that goes out of the natural environment eventually comes back in. Understanding this rule provides the basis for the recycling decisions in the household.

"In *technological* recycling we obviously do not get rid of materials, we simply restructure them and retain them *within* the production economy. In *natural* recycling we depend on the natural environment to close the material loop" (Koenig, 1973, p. 4). Families need to understand the interdependence of the human built and natural environments as they make consumer choices that either enhance or constrain recycling potentials. A central concern is that the natural system not be overloaded or "overdriven" and rendered incapable of processing materials.

Through the growth in technology, humans have been able to fashion from the natural environment a large number of alternative products that have made possible diversified styles of living. This has both enhanced and restricted the quality of life in the family, creating basic conflicts between systems.

Every gain is won at some cost. Historically humans have been accustomed to thinking of natural environment resources as inexhaustible. Shortages of fossil fuels and food in recent times have forced us to recognize the need for replacing what is drawn from our global environment. We are confronted with the question of weighing costs. Technology enables us to have more and larger automobiles, but automobile exhausts pollute our atmosphere, making our air unhealthy to breathe. Automobiles also use fossil fuels, which are in limited supply. At the same time, the automobile has made people highly mobile, thus expanding alternatives.

Must we alter our environment in ways that may be dangerous to our health, or are we concerned with improving the quality of life? To what extent is scarcity a psychological and cultural concept rather than a physical or biological one? "Real" shortages "depend upon the wants and ends we choose to honor as well as the technology and capabilities we can harness to expand the means. To this extent, the problem is ultimately ethical, relying more on our choice of values . . . " (Hazard, 1975, p. 39).

People have created particular environments that are sources of rules and policies that regulate the activities between people and the natural environment, between human groups in family, school, community, and national settings, and between social, political, judicial, and economic units themselves. Through these controlled feedback systems (cybernetic), humans can, on the basis of information and understanding, determine the direction the system will take. It is because people can control these systems that they can choose and hence design alternative futures. The rules of regulatory systems are not inherent to the system. They are devised by people and can be changed or adapted by them. Determining these fundamental "rules of behaving" is our central decision making task. The family plays a major role in educating its members to create and use these rules.


## ENVIRONMENTAL FACTORS AFFECTING CHOICE

Wise choices depend on how aware families are of what is feasible and acceptable in the environments with which they interact. Elbing

(1970, pp. 502-514) has developed a model for viewing decision making in interaction situations from an historical perspective. The Elbing model clarifies the numerous forces that interact in decision making, emphasizing the historical significance of past decision situations. The model is appropriate for families because it focuses on

decisions which are made in interaction situations, in contrast to those which judiciously can be made unilaterally. The interaction decisions are those made in situations where two or more parties are negotiating, bargaining, or competing on an interpersonal or intergroup basis, and where fore the various parties, the decisions usually are not mutually exclusive events. In such situations, the decision of one party cannot be made independent of considering the decisions of the other party or parties.*

In constructing his model Elbing specified three criteria: (1) the decisions must be viewed in terms of the situation at the time of decision rather than solely in terms of meaningful subsequent events; (2) the separate views, perceptions, or anticipations of the various persons involved must be considered; and (3) environmental factors must be included even if the participants are not aware of them and even though they can only be perceived from a broad chronological or geographical vantage point.

Figure 8 shows Elbing's representation of an interaction choice situation, with the decision problem being indicated by the square $ABCD$. Area $X$ is the total psychological makeup of one person and area $Y$ is that of the other person. Each person has a different perception of the problem with overlap in only part of the problem area. Although the individual perceptions of $X$ and $Y$ cover a large part of the problem, $ABCD$, part of the problem area lies beyond their perceptions (emphasizing the limitations and selective effects of human perception).

Environmental forces, $Z$, include the natural and human environment existing when the decision is being made, that is, the physical, social, political, and economic conditions existing at the time. Area $Z$ dictates the boundaries of possible decision alternatives. Each indi-

*From Behavioral Decisions in Organizations by Alvar O. Elbing Copyright © 1970 by Scott, Foresman and Company. Reprinted by permission of the publisher.

MODEL FOR VIEWING ALTERNATIVES IN A FAMILY DECISION SITUATION**

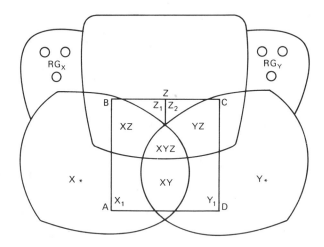

**Figure 8.** Model For Viewing Alternatives in a Family Decision Situation.**

$ABCD$ - Family decision situation
  $X$ - Family member
  $Y$ - Family member
  $Z$ - environment
$RG_x$ - reference group for member $X$
$RG_y$ - reference group for member $Y$
$XZ$ - alternatives perceived by $X$ and acceptable in existing environment
$YZ$ - alternatives perceived by $Y$ and acceptable in existing environment

$XY$ - Alternatives perceived by both $X$ and $Y$ but *not* acceptable in the environment.
$X_1$ and $Y_1$ - Alternatives perceived by one member but not acceptable in the environment.
$Z_1$ and $Z_2$ - Acceptable alternatives not perceived by family members.
$XYZ$ - Alternatives perceived by both family members and acceptable in the environment.

vidual perceives certain alternatives as existing in the environment and as being acceptable social behavior ($xz$ and $yz$). Some alternatives acceptable to both $X$ and $Y$ ($xy$) are viewed as not acceptable in the environment. Acceptable alternatives exist that are not perceived by either $X$ or $Y$ ($z_1$). Some potentially acceptable alternatives ($z_2$) are influencing the situation but they can only be under-

* Could be expanded to include more family members.
** Adapted from Alvar O. Elbing, Jr., "A Model for Viewing Decision Making in Interaction Situations form an Historical Perspective." in Alvar Elbing, *Behavioral Decisions in Organizations.* Copyright © 1970 by Scott, Foresman and Company. Reprinted by permission of the publisher.

stood from a different historical, geographic, or psychological vantage point. Elbing points out that environmental factors affect the decision situation and the manner in which it can be perceived. In addition, the individual's entire personality may be influenced by groups to which he or she belongs: "Individual attitudes and resulting behavior reflect the norms and values of groups to which the individuals refer" (Elbing, 1970, p. 511). Reference groups ($RGX$ and $RGY$) for either person might include groups where one is a member (such as school or occupational groups), groups that one aspires to join (such as a club), or disassociative groups (such as peer groups) from which one would like to withdraw. Reference groups help shape one's perception of a situation.

To help clarify the Elbing model, a brief description of a fictional family follows:

### Hernandez Family*

Early last month in Brownsville, Texas, the Hernandez family began to prepare for their annual summer trip. It was to be an extended trip — they would drive over 10,000 miles and pass through a dozen states in the coming six months.

To some people this would sound like a pleasurable vacation, but to the Hernandez family it is a way of life, they are migrant farm laborers. The family spends half the year traveling from job to job and the other six months in Texas where employment is very limited.

But this year was different. Word had come that the lettuce crops in Colorado had frozen, fruit in Utah was to be harvested mechanically, and migrant housing in Montana and Wyoming had been condemned. Jobs would be very difficult to find this year.

Maria Hernandez felt that the family should stay in Texas. If they did, the children could continue in school for the remainder of the year and they wouldn't have to risk finding no work. Although their house in Brownsville was small, at least it was a roof over their heads, Maria felt. Also her family lives in the community and have helped Maria's family at times.

Lalo Hernandez felt the family must go. He had been a migrant worker all his life and this was all he knew. His friends had told him that rumors that there were no jobs were not true—there had always been jobs in years past. Lalo wishes permanent work existed for him in Brownsville so that he could stay in the area but his skills are limited to agricultural chores. Besides if the family stayed in Texas how would they make a living?

Lalo was a little concerned whether his truck would make the journey.

*Developed by Kenneth Slater, Graduate Assistant, Department of Family Ecology, Michigan State University, 1970.

The 1956 Ford pickup with 125,000 miles on it was in need of new tires. Lalo's brother thought they might not have enough money for gasoline, since there would be no welfare check while they were traveling. Because of this Lalo's brother also feels that the family should stay in Texas.

Last week Maria saw a notice in the grocery store announcing a new training program offered by the Texas Migrant Labor Board. The program was designed to help migrants escape the migrant stream by teaching them new skills and pays a stipend while a person is in training. A worker for the board told her he thought the family would qualify for the program. When Maria told Lalo about the program, he was interested but wondered if he'd find a job after he completed the training.

Using the Elbing Model, the following factors can be identified:

1. $ABCD$—the decision problem
2. $X$ and $Y$ — the decision makers
3. The environmental factors
4. $RG_x$ and $RG_y$ — the reference groups for $X$ and $Y$, respectively.
5. $XZ$ and $YZ$ — alternative perceived by $X$ and acceptable to the environment; by $Y$
6. $XY$ — alternatives perceived by both $X$ and $Y$ but not acceptable to the environment
7. $X_1Y_1$ — alternatives perceived by one party but not acceptable to the environment
8. Socially acceptable alternatives are not perceived by either party $-Z_1$
9. $Z_2$ — alternatives not perceivable at that time
10. $XYZ$ — alternatives perceived by both parties and acceptable to the environment

Analysis and identification of various factors and how they affect the Hernandez decision situation illustrates how alternatives for a particular family are expanded or limited by the environment. Use of the Elbing model also clarifies the interaction of family members in a decision situation, and it implies that an increase in the number of members involved leads to a decrease in the number of shared alternatives acceptable ($XYZ$) in the environment.

## INFLUENCE OF NATURAL ENVIRONMENT

The physical environment expands or limits the alternatives open to families. The form, quantity, and availability of energy sources determine possible alternatives. Families living in areas that have distinct seasons, including harsh winters, are limited by these climatic boundaries. Families who live near an ocean or lake have different alternatives open to them than families living in a desert community. Residents of a mountain resort area may have opportunities unavailable to families living at sea level, but they also have restrictions.

To some extent a family can control the effects of physical environment factors. For example, if a river is known to overflow its banks after heavy rain or snow, local citizens can seek the cooperation of government officials to help prevent future disasters. The effects of hurricanes, tornadoes, and earthquakes may be less subject to control. Although certain geographic areas are known to be subject to such natural disasters, who can predict when a severe earthquake or other natural disaster might occur and which homes might be destroyed by it? A family may decide to continue living in an earthquake-prone area because the father has a good job in that community, relatives and friends are near, and chance that their house will not be lost. On the other hand, some families decide that any such risk is too great and they move to a geographical area with fewer risk factors.

Certain geographic elements of the immediate environment can be controlled by the family. For instance, the family can choose to live in a cold climate and select clothing and housing to protect them from the elements. They may choose to plant grass and maintain a beautiful lawn around the house or may use decorative stones in lieu of doing so much yard work. Each choice has both a cost and a benefit.

Another effect is related to geographic elements. Land, its scarcity and productivity in large measure determines the availability of food, a basic resource. Because people have unwittingly raped nature through overusing land, redesigning terrain by building dams or depleting forests, some land has become nonfunctional for food production. Add to this the climatic factors of too little or too much rainfall and one can quickly sense how the natural environment sharply influences decisions.

Health decisions may be related to geographic conditions. Sometimes families may decide to move in order to escape the harmful effects of smog, snow shoveling, humidity, or other natural effects of their environment. The quiet, relaxing life of a small community may be sought to replace the fast pace and busy traffic of a metropolitan area. On the other hand, the variety and quality of medical services may attract a family from an isolated area to a large community.

The physical environment of the family must be considered in relation to social and economic factors. Life on a farm in the twentieth century is quite different from what it was 50 years ago. Grapes may still be the principal agricultural commodity, but methods of caring for the vineyard and harvesting the fruit have changed. Through irrigation and fertilization the landscape has changed. Urban ways of living have spread to rural areas resulting in less isolation than once existed, in large measure because of mass transportation and communication. Both farm and urban families have more alternatives open to them as a result of industrialization.

Restrictions are imposed by living in a particular community. From an economic standpoint one might consider what happens to families when the main industry of a community is wiped out. How mobile does a family feel after having lived in a small community, with a unique geographic and climatic environment, for 50 years or more? Is it easy for such a family to hold an image of a better life that would be sufficiently strong to make the sacrifices worthwhile to obtain it?

Refugees and immigrants from other countries seem to be drawn to certain parts of the United States by climate or economic conditions. Although many of these families disperse to other areas, some communities have pockets where particular ethnic groups have settled. Despite efforts to desegregate housing, racial prejudice is still a powerful force in certain communities. How well are families from heterogeneous backgrounds able to mix? What are local communities doing to build wholesome relationships? An analysis of where revolutionary movements have started would indicate that physical setting is at least an incidental factor in radical social change.

The natural environment holds the key to all sources of energy. Food resources to support any population level are inextricably linked to the energy sources in the natural environment. Ultimately, technology to support any population size is also dependent on energy resources in the natural environment.

## Influences of Technological Environment

Technological developments can exert great influence on the resources and well-being of families. Cheap and efficient means of converting energy could ease shortages in areas where utilities are scarce. We have seen the development of automobiles into high-powered, gas-eating polluters of the environment. We have learned to enjoy the convenience of frost-free refrigerators, garbage disposals, air conditioners, and other home equipment that increase our uses of utilities. Ecologists are questioning how many of the things we own or think we want are essential to our well-being and, more importantly, what the real cost of the goods might be to the natural environment and to society.

Technology has made it possible for more family members to work outside the home. Not only has there been an expansion in available jobs, but services once performed by the family have become available in the marketplace, such as ready-prepared food and clothing, counseling and child-care services. The economic system interacting with the production system opens employment opportunities for family members. These new opportunities force the family to adapt home life to fit the reduced time and energy family members have available for family use.

With the variety of mechanical aids available for the home, particularly in the kitchen and laundry, the home could become a status symbol. Undoubtedly some families buy features on their appliances without being aware of their true needs and the cost. Impressing a friend or "keeping up with the Joneses" is a powerful environmental influence. For example, a retired couple built a new house in an expensive area of a city where all of the houses had to have a substantial minimum square footage. Although this couple did not need a wet bar for serving alcoholic beverages, the architect advised them to install one because the house would have greater resale value in future years when that couple might wish to sell. Most prospective buyers of houses in that area expect to find a bar already installed.

Every day radio, television, and newspapers remind a tremendous number of families that there is a world different from the one in which they live. For some, this awareness causes discontent and a determination to copy, at least in part, what is seen. Their efforts may result in better schools, more police protection, more adequate medical care, less pollution, or other benefits. On the other hand, families sometimes misdirect their efforts toward acquiring products or features that have no real utility for them. Communication through the mass media can change the family's objectives, expand their vision, open more alternatives, and cause them to behave differently.

Because of technological advancements, our society has become energy intensive rather than labor intensive. Technology has the potential to obscure our ties to the natural system. The implications of this, both socially and economically, may result in an unawareness of the costs of technology, while emphasizing the benefits. Dependence on energy will affect alternatives available to families in the technological arena.

### Influences of Regulatory Systems

The regulatory systems are created by humans to control in some fashion the relationships between humans and the natural environment. Through social, economic, political, religious, educational, and family systems, processes of production, consumption, and socialization guide the flow of matter-energy and information between people and environment.

Economic systems create "laws" of supply, demand, and distribution of resources. These laws influence decisions. Economic conditions in a nation and in the world have a marked effect not only on the decisions made by government officials but also on those made by individuals and families. Financial news reports link sharp rises or declines in the stock market to such occasions as a president's illness, changes in interest rates, or devaluation of the dollar. Many times it is almost impossible to offer a rational explanation for some of the factors that affect the market. Who can predict the decisions small investors will make? Yet, the economic well-being of the family can be affected by the whims of many other families who may suddenly decide to sell their mutual funds, pull out of the stock market, or invest in foreign currency.

Many of the economic decisions made by government officials affect families directly or indirectly. A government health program opens new possibilities for decisions regarding health and medical care and use of financial resources within families. Changes in interest rates influence whether or not a family can consider purchasing a house or condominium. Funds allocated for child care make it possible for many women to seek job training and employment outside the home. Legislative controls, such as farm subsidies and price freezing, affect the economic position of families as consumers. Legislation regarding economic matters can either restrict a family's choices or extend their alternatives. The impact of economic conditions on family decisions is felt especially strongly when a particular resource, such as energy derived from fossil fuels, is scarce or during times of high inflation or unemployment.

Many families are existing under conditions that do not fulfill minimal requirements for living. These pockets of extreme poverty often are in the midst of an affluent society. Rivlin (1975, p. 4) has stated that

> Real incomes have been rising over the years at respectable if not spectacular rates, but measures of inequality have hardly changed since World War II . . . . The bottom 20 percent of families gets 5 percent of total income and the top 20 percent gets a little more than 40 percent—the numbers have hardly varied at all since the late 1940's.

Suggestions that the rich should share their wealth with the poor are very controversial in nations where individual initiative is valued.

As a result of a country's favorable economic position, families can be bombarded with a vast array of products, many of which are new and not tested adequately. Families are constantly urged to buy products they neither need, want, or can afford. Many persons earn their living by dreaming up ways of attracting consumers to discard what they have and buy a new model of a different color, shape, size, height, or some other unimportant variation of a material good.

We can describe social and economic development as moving through four phases: traditional, modernizing or industrializing, industrial, and postindustrial. Technological development, with its continually increasing production of material goods, is the most important characteristic of modernization. Increased production of goods increases options and complexity. Industrialization brings a complex division of labor, changes in occupational and family roles, and competition for the more financially rewarding occupational roles. As development progresses, a greater number of choices become available and concern for private rights increases. The potential for conflict in values becomes apparent.

An explanation of the relationship between self-interest and social conflict was offered by Tallman (1972, p. 3):

It seems plausible that the drive people have for greater material well-being increases a collective push for more production, a process which in turn increases both the efficiency and complexity of the social structure. As the social structure grows in complexity, available choices grow; as role choices increase, expectations (particularly inter-generational expectations) increase; and as expectations increase those in the more deprived positions of the structure anticipate, at least for their children, greater opportunities for occupational mobility and material rewards. If this is to occur, the norms of distributive justice must become more egalitarian and sanction increasingly open competition for the more highly rewarded offices.

Since there is a strong tendency for "haves" to want to protect their privileged position against incursions, equal opportunities rarely exist within any society. With development, therefore, there is a situation where even though increased choices occur there remains a gap between expectations and the rewards available to large numbers of people. This gap is the basis of "relative deprivation" and provides the impetus for continued pressure toward change. There is considerable data which suggests that relative deprivation, rather than objective social conditions, represents the essential conditions for political unrest and subsequent social change.*

Relative deprivation is the sense of imbalance families feel when radio, television, reading, and physical mobility reveal life styles different from their own. Through exposure to mass media and mobility, then, families begin to form images of what could or should be; images that are often in painful contrast to the reality of the family's present situation. Consequently, as modernization or technological advances take place in society, more and more families experience conflict between what they have and what they think should exist in their community. This gap leads to feelings of alienation from other people.

Opportunities are available to the family within the economic system. The system provides material payoffs in exchange for investments of individual resources of family members. The payoffs shift with such variables as supply and demand, changes in power distribution, and shifting interests. The hope is for an optimal return, but re-

*From "Social Structure and Socialization for Change" by Irving Tallman.

turn is not always governed by the norms of distributive justice. A high value is placed on the accumulation of material goods. As production increases, people demand more goods and services. More energy in the form of both natural resources and information is necessary. More information is needed to cope with the complex environment that new options have generated.

Schroder et al. (1967, p. 31) hypothesizes a U-curve relationship between environmental complexity and level of information needed:

> overly simple environments . . . fail to present sufficiently diverse units of dimensional information, fail to stimulate the processes of integration—that is, simple . . . (levels of integration) are sufficient for coping with such environments. Overly complex environments, which provide excessively diverse and/or numerous dimensional units of information, reduce the generation of integratively complex rules for processing information and also reduce the level of integration and differentiation involved.*

Highly industrialized societies generate vast amounts of information, larger numbers of available choices, and a corresponding increase in the rate of change. According to the U-curve, structures can develop beyond the optimal level, resulting in a decline in the generation of new knowledge and retardation of development. This condition may characterize the postindustrialized societies.

When people are satiated with material goods, truly radical innovation can occur. Value shifts can occur that involve the enhancement of alternative life styles. Many radical solutions that call for simplifying family structures, if coupled with an antiscientific orientation, could limit the generation of new knowledge. Some solutions would break down bureaucratic structures and increase participatory democracy and private family autonomy. Simplistic systems of knowledge, mysticism, and nonmaterialistic goals are growing in appeal. The solutions being generated call for less complex social structures and implicitly require a more communal and less individualistic orientation.

*From *Human Information Processing: Individuals and Groups Functioning in Complex Social Situations* by Harold M. Schroder, Michael Driver, and Siegfried Streufert. Copyright © 1967 by Holt, Rinehart and Winston, Inc. Reprinted by permission of Holt, Rinehart and Winston.

The larger social structure is interpreted and mediated through the family, with the greatest impact coming through the occupational roles occupied by family members. Tallman (1972, p. 10) suggests that "the experiences of the role occupant in achieving his ends (i.e., the number of available choices, the cost-reward of his efforts, the amount of information he must assimilate and generate, the level of concreteness at which he works) –all have their correlaries in family behavior and in the orientation of offspring."

Kohn (1969) demonstrates the centrality of occupational roles in determining the values, attitudes, and behavior of family members:

Occupational experiences . . . permeate men's views, not only of work and their role in work, but of the world and of the self. The conditions of occupational life at higher social class levels facilitate interest in the intrinsic qualities of the job, foster a view of self and society that is conducive to believing in the possibilities of rational action toward purposive goals and promote the valuation of self-direction. The conditions of occupational life at lower social class levels limits men's view of a job primarily to the extrinsic benefits it provides, fosters a narrowly circumscribed conception of self in society, and promotes the positive valuation of conformity to authority. Conditions of work that foster thought and initiative tend to enlarge man's conceptions of reality, conditions of constraint tend to narrow them (p. 192).

Closely supervised men tend not only to value conformity for their children, but also to emphasize extrinsic benefits that jobs provide rather than opportunities for intrinsic accomplishment, to have standards of morality keyed to the letter rather than the spirit of the law, to be distrustful, to be resistant to innovation and change, to lack self-confidence, and to be anxious . . . .

Men who work at complexly organized jobs, in addition to valuing self-direction for children, tend to emphasize intrinsic aspects of the job, to be open-minded and tolerant of non-conformity, to have moral standards that demand more than conformity to the letter of the law, to be receptive to change, and not to be self-deprecatory (pp. 166–67).*

What opportunity does a community offer its residents to participate in decisions that affect the majority of families? Opportunities

*From *Class and Conformity* by Melvin Kohn.

may be there, but if families do not believe that they can make a difference, they probably will not become involved. The public choices made, however, will have an impact on their private choices. Clark (1968, p. 37) describes four types of community decision making structures that afford different levels of family involvement:

1. *Mass participation model.* Members of the community are highly active in all types of decisions. There is little vertical differentiation between the "people" and the leaders.
2. *Monolithic model.* A small number of persons, who are at the top of the hierarchy, influence nearly all issues.
3. *Polylithic model.* Within each separate issue area (e.g., housing, recreation), there is a monolithic structure whose leaders vary from one issue to another.
4. *Pluralistic model.* Within each issue area, most decisions are made by undifferentiated clusters of persons specializing in the different issue areas.

Different concepts of power are implicit in these four models. In regard to the political conditions of a community, we might think of power as the potential ability of individuals and families to select, change, and attain the goals of a given social system. Can the difference in the distribution of power among the four decision-making structures be identified? When family members perceive themselves to be at the bottom of a monolithic structure, they are likely to feel powerless. In a pluralistic model, family members might become involved with certain issues where they can see their influence is helping to bring about changes.

The community may be conceived as an energy system comprised of relationships among functionally differentiated units, each of which has the ability to influence the family decision making process. Each unit (e.g., family, church) is an organization of power for the conduct of its function. Performance of any one part affects the conditions under which other parts or subsystems can carry out their functions. An almost continuous interplay of influence occurs. Power is expressed in two ways: (1) functional—required to carry out a function; (2) derivative—spills over into external relationships, regulating the interaction between parts.

As an example of how the family fits into the community power structure, consider one of the family's functions—concern for the safety of its children. If a store features toys that are unsafe, the parents can fulfill their function by not buying those toys for the children and not allowing such toys to be available where their children play. Their influence can extend to another subsystem when they speak to the store manager about the dangers inherent in the toys. Their influence can even affect the system as a whole if they notify the Department of Consumer Affairs or some other government division that can take the necessary action to prevent other parts of the subsystem from suffering future harm.

Many government agencies enforce laws relating to consumer protection. Although they may not be able to represent an individual consumer, they can offer advice, information, or appropriate referrals. When a family feels that a business or professional person has deliberately misled or cheated one of its members, pressure from a government agency may bring results. Recognizing the frustration an individual consumer experiences when trying to cut the "red tape" of complex government structures, ombudsman offices are available in some communities.

What can a family reasonably expect from government? Services would be high on the list. Services include such things as fire and police protection, public schools, adult education opportunities, parks, and recreational facilities. Some forward-looking governments recognize the need for adequate legal representation, perhaps including plans for prepaid legal services and consumer consultation.

Licensing, registration, and certification are other functions that families can expect from government. Licenses to operate a business may be granted simply upon receipt of an application and payment of a fee. Professional qualifications may be examined before granting licenses to physicians and nurses. Usually the standards for qualification are minimal and the government may not have adequate resources to see that standards are enforced.

Governments may also protect property rights; for example, if a new state highway will cut across a family's property, that family has a right to "fair" compensation. As one focuses on how the external environment can affect a family's decisions, consideration can be given to the various alternatives open to a family whose home would be in the way or adjacent to a new freeway. Undoubtedly, the family's freedom to make decisions would be affected by a forced move.

The judicial system also influences the family decision arena. Products normally used may be declared unsafe by court action and removed from the market, altering family consumption patterns, i.e.

the diabetic who once used products with artificial sweeteners may not be able to purchase them, as a result of court rulings. Women may find certain brands of birth control pills no longer available. Farmers and amateur gardeners have to adjust their growing plans as a result of court decisions removing certain insecticides from the market.

The rights of individuals and groups have been affected by judicial rulings, particularly in antidiscrimination decisions, which allow increased alternatives for many. Some families have found alternatives reduced as a result of court action. When a family member is in prison, the rest of the family must adjust, often on severely restricted financial resources.

Court actions affecting employers and producers have an impact on a family's spendable income and on choices open to it. Judicial decisions may permeate every decision area for families and can create or diminish alternatives.

The political atmosphere can have a great influence on the social setting for a family. The possible effects on a given community when changes or exceptions to zoning regulations are granted are many. Imagine what it would be like for a family to move from a tenement into a multistory, integrated, urban renewal project complete with laundry facilities and playground. Perhaps for some families the burden of new choices would be overwhelming. Not to be overlooked are the constraints that a high-rise might place on a family's decision about such amenities as play space for children, and nearness to friends and extended family. Both types of living space, the tenement or the high-rise, influence choices.

A family who bought a single-family house may find high-rise apartment buildings in the next block within a few years. Street parking in front of a family's house may become impossible when a theater, school, or hospital opens nearby. Such changes in the neighborhood may force the family choosing to remain in that community to adopt a different life style, or they may accelerate a move from that community.

The political process essentially acts to maintain the equilibrium in a system. One kind of tax may be lowered and another replaces it. The budget is reduced in one respect in order to give priority to another project. Energy production must be stimulated while energy consumption must be depressed. Economic growth must be fostered while preserving environmental health. A master plan must be developed as the basis for future land use, coastal protection, power plant siting, and other aspects pertinent to the development and conservation of natural resources. These and many other decisions made by the power structure of the external environment significantly influence the family's quality of life.

The goals of society and of various social classes, communities, and individuals often overlap. For example, the goals of a wide cross-section of American society are likely to include a free choice of housing and jobs, continuity of employment, opportunities for leisure and recreation, free choice of education, unpolluted air, mobility, privacy, security, excitement, beauty, and some contact with nature. Families differ in the extent to which they need any of these human desires, and in the priorities they place on them. Family desires and the fulfillment of expectations are in constant interplay with forces of the external environment—social setting, political atmosphere, geographic conditions, technological factors, and economic influences. Likewise, these elements interact with each other so the family's external environment is a dynamic force that both affects and is affected by the individuals and subgroups comprising the total environment.

Gordon (1964, p. 160) describes American society as a "mosaic of ethnic groups based on race, religion, and to a declining extent, national origins, criss-crossed by social class stratification to form the characteristic subsocietal unit, the ethclass." Any number of racial and national groups might be included, but the influence of gangs, clubs, neighborhoods, work groups, and special interest clubs with whom individual family members spend a portion of their time all influence choice.

Cultural differences are an enriching, yet often misunderstood, part of American life. By culture we mean that set of habitual and traditional ways of thinking and responding which characterizes a particular group at a given time. Beliefs, customs, food habits, artistic norms, and other feelings or thought patterns are a legacy from society. Each subsystem has a "way of life" that distinguishes it from other groups. Just as personality is unique to an individual, culture is the heart of the social environment. Culture is made up of material and nonmaterial traits which are products of learned behavior.

Diamond et al. (1963) uses two terms that describe the significant effects of the imprint of culture:

*Cultural imprinting* represents a process by which an initial disposition to respond positively to any object of a given class becomes quickly narrowed, so that it is available only to one member of that class . . . . It is the simultaneous strengthening of a disposition to respond positively to one stimulus and the active extinction, before decay otherwise would set in, of an original disposition to respond similarly to many other stimuli . . . .

*Canalization* (the progressive shifts in differential response to the various means of satisfying a drive) eliminates untried paths which intrinsically are as good as those that come to be frequented . . . . We become accustomed to a national diet and therefore reject strange foods as unpalatable . . . . One does not simply learn to like rice and potatoes; one also acquires . . . a reduced readiness to consume and enjoy the untried. Choice . . . appears as a rivalry between appetites which cannot be simultaneously satisfied (Diamond, pp. 143-145).

Culture is an adaptive mechanism, providing ready-made solutions to the problems encountered by the group. Social patterns are not inherently right or wrong, but observance of customs by everyone makes large areas of life predictable. Culture has form and pattern; it gives a group a certain style of life that is peculiarly its own. By using examples from a variety of cultures, Lee (1959) illustrates differences in members views of individual autonomy, personal significance and group structure, responsibility, dietary choice, and other areas that influence families.

Cultural pluralism—the many religious, racial, and nationality patterns coexisting in a society—is expressed in American society by those subgroups who retain their identity and aspects of their parent culture. However, Gordon (1964, p. 52) points out that social class differences more strongly influence cultural behavior than do ethnic differences. Social class differences are generally based on differing amounts of income and education. People of the same social class tend to have similar values and behavior even though their ethnic backgrounds differ; those from different social classes act differently even if they have the same ethnic background.

Davis (1965, pp. 231-232) says "cultural deprivation" is a misnomer:

All human groups, and members of groups have a very complex, and strongly sanctioned culture—language, child-rearing practices, sexual controls, kinship relationships, parent-child and superhuman-human relationships. The *low-income* groups . . . have, in fact, cultural patterns of behavior, values, and learned emotions, which organize all the major areas of behavior mentioned . . . . Children of the poor . . . already have learned a complex change-resistant system of culture, a *survival system*, before they enter the kindergarten or first grade . . . . [They] are disadvantaged in our economy, in our schools, and in our social system, because they have to learn a new cultural pattern of behavior, including: (1) habits of speech, writing, use of books and other skills; and (2) new modes of sublimating or socializing the sexual, acquisitive, and aggressive drives which middle-class children and adolescents learn in their families.*

Stereotypes destroy our understanding by causing us to see pictures that may or may not correspond with reality, yet they are the basis for many of our judgments and actions regarding another cultural group. Stereotypes can be debilitating; they can shape negative images and limited social roles for the group they describe.

Prejudice is a way of conveying meaning and an image that disparages and implies contempt for another social group. The dominant group can set standards for physical appearance, cultural values, and social behavior. Prejudice has deep roots in American society and most victims of prejudice are also victims of negative stereotyping. The manifestations of prejudice in discriminatory behavior are damaging to many individuals and families of minority groups. Some members of victimized groups suffer loss of self-esteem with a resulting hidden self-contempt. Some withdraw defensively into their own selves or social group. Some defensive feelings lead to aggression, hostility, and other offensive behavior. Society as a whole experiences social conflict and a resulting loss of civic unity.

Many American communities are seeking ways to conserve the value of cultural differences while encouraging various minority and majority groups to learn how to live together cooperatively. Some families adapt to cultural differences in a passive manner—they un-

*From Allison Davis, "Cultural Patterns in Remediation," *Educational Horizons*, 43, 4 (1965): 231-232.

consciously or deliberately subordinate themselves to their environment. Toleration, an early state of accommodation, enables a family to be "polite" and put up with what cannot be avoided but to continue disliking it. Active adaptation, on the other hand, involves the family in efforts to create a more humanistic environment or to change themselves in relation to the environment.

## ALIENATION

Yablonsky (1972, p. xiii) sees dehumanization and anomie as a "robopathic condition of social death . . . . People may in a subtle fashion become robot-like in their interaction and become human robots, or robopaths." "Robopaths" combines the two words, "robot" and "pathology." As machines take on more human tasks, people seem to become more like machines. People are becoming "locked in robot-like interaction in human groups that have become social machines." Humanistic values and contact with reality disappear and a sense of helplessness pervades the culture. Robopathic behavior is ritualistic, past-oriented, conforming, image-involved, lacking compassion, hostile, self-righteous, and alienated. It exists in all people and in all societies. It limits capacity to choose.

In our highly industrialized society it is necessary that people cooperate smoothly in groups and are willing to be told what to do. Our economy depends on consumers whose tastes are standardized and who can be influenced easily to consume more. Consumers are alienated from the things with which they are surrounded, knowing little of how they originated and developed. Much of our recreation is passive; we enjoy sports, movies, musicals, or other leisure pursuits in which we are alienated from the actors. Fromm (1955, p. 270) alerts us to the psychological results of alienation: "Man regresses to a receptive and marketing orientation and ceases to be productive; he loses his sense of self, becomes dependent on approval, hence tends to conform and yet to feel insecure; he is dissatisfied, bored, and anxious, and spends most of his energy attempting to compensate or cover up this anxiety."*

Anomie is a feeling of rootlessness, of being cut off, or not be-

*From *The Sane Society* by Erich Fromm. Copyright © 1955 by Erich Fromm. Reprinted by permission of Holt, Rinehart and Winston, Publishers.

longing to other parts of society. Anomie reflects the confusion which results when a lack of identity with a coherent system of norms and values exists and feelings of forced conformity prevail. Social disorganization can result from an anomic trend where external restraints are viewed as intolerable limitations on one's personal rights and internal restraints are weakly developed.

Bronfenbrenner (1974, p. 53) views the impact of environments on families as a major source of alienation. In a multi-alternative environment families must make numerous and rapid choices. Too often the changes to which they must adjust are based on unseen forces rather than deliberated choice. The direction of change is that of disorganization rather than organized new direction. The family, lacking an anchor of relevance, becomes isolated from its environment—rootless and unconnected.

Rootlessness and feelings of unconnectedness stem from living in a world of continuous change. Part of this change results from family mobility; when they move to a completely different area, families must adjust to a new social setting. Some change occurs simply because of cyclic family development. As individual members of the family grow older, they develop new interests that often extend the social circles in which they move. Communities themselves change as families move in and out, as schools and other institutions reach toward new goals, as industry expands or closes, and as government officials seek new ways of making the community attractive. Our highly mobile society includes migrant workers, servicemen, students who go away to college, families who travel with campers, senior citizens who move to retirement communities, and others who flee to escape the city and racial integration. A "family of torn roots" leaves a legacy of coldness and a sense of loneliness to members who are uprooted. Change and mobility can lead to alienation.

Change and mobility also have advantages. Gans (1972, p. 28) has a much more optimistic view of mobility:

Traditional patterns of social life based on kinship, ethnicity, and shared turf are being complemented by—and sometimes replaced with—a social life based on shared cultural and other interests. This shift is the very basis of social life—from who one is to what one does—is not new, and it is not caused by mobility, but it is particularly visible in the new suburbs, college and retirement communities, singles projects, and wherever else previous strangers come together to create a new social life . . . . All the reliable studies of communities in which it is happening indicate that rates of loneliness and pathology are very low and that satisfaction is great.

True, one effect of a mutual-interest-based social life has been the increasing homogeneity, by age and class, of modern American communities, but the historical record suggests that in the past, heterogeneous people lived together by necessity rather than by choice, and that as soon as affluence and opportunities for mobility enabled them to choose, they headed for more homogeneous surroundings (and not only in the suburbs) . . . .*

## SUMMARY

Families exist in a given time and space, surrounded by an environment that provides an infinite number of alternatives. The capacity of the family to identify feasible alternatives is constrained or enhanced by the degree to which the environment is perceived as generating possible alternatives. No decision is made in isolation, each has a past and a future. To a large extent the values underlying their choices and the alternatives they select, shape the futures of families. Selection is rooted in an understanding of how environments influence the possible alternatives.

## SELECTED REFERENCES

Bronfenbrenner, Urie. "The Origins of Alienation." *Scientific American.* 230 (August 1974): 53–61.

Clark, Terry N. (ed.) *Community Structure and Decision-Making: Comparative Analyses.* San Francisco: Chandler Publishing, 1968.

Davis, Allison. "Cultural Patterns in Remediation" *Educational Horizons.* 43 (Summer, 1965): 231–51.

Diamond, Solomon, Richard S. Balvin, and Florence R. Diamond. *Inhibition and Choice.* New York: Harper & Row, 1963.

*Herbert J. Gans, "Vance Packard Misperceives the Way Most American Movers Live." Copyright © 1972 Ziff-Davis Publishing Company. Reprinted by permission of *Psychology Today* magazine.

Elbing, Alvar O. Jr., "A Model for Viewing Decision Making in Interaction Situations from an Historical Perspective." In Alvar Elbing (ed.) *Behavioral Decisions in Organizations.* Glenview, Ill.: Scott, Foresman, 1970, pp. 502–514.

Fromm, Eric. *The Sane Society.* New York: Rinehart, 1955.

Gans, Herbert J. "Vance Packard Misperceives the Way Most American Movers Live." *Psychology Today,* 6 (September, 1972): 20–28.

Gordon, Milton. *Assimilation in American Life.* New York: Oxford University Press. 1964.

Hazard, John I. "Energy and Transportation." *Phi Kappa Phi Journal.* LV, 1 (Winter, 1975): p. 39.

Koenig, Herman. "The Life Support System in Relation to the Natural Environment." Unpublished paper presented to Extension Home Economists, November 26, 1973 (mimeo.). East Lansing, Mich., pp. 2 and 4.

Koenig, Herman E., Thomas Edens, and W. Cooper. "Ecology, Engineering and Economics." *Proceedings of the IEEE.* 63 (March 1975): 501–511.

Koenig, Herman, and Thomas C. Edens. "Energy, Ecology and Economics: The Realities of Thermodynamically Based Economics." Unpublished paper, September 22, 1975. Departments of Electrical Engineering and Systems Science and Agricultural Economics, Michigan State University, East Lansing, Mich.

Kohn, Melvin. *Class and Conformity.* Homewood, Ill.: The Dorsey Press, 1969, pp. 166–167 and 192.

Lee, Dorothy. *Freedom and Culture.* Englewood Cliffs, N.J.: Prentice-Hall, 1959.

Paolucci, Beatrice, and M. Janice Hogan. "The Energy Crisis and the Family." *Journal of Home Economics.* 65 (December 1973): 12–15.

Rivlin, Alice M. "Income Distribution—Can Economists Help?" *American Economic Review.* 65 (May 1975): 1–15.

Shroder, Harold, M. J. Driver, and S. Streufert. *Human Information Processing.* New York: Holt, Rinehart and Winston, 1967.

Tallman, Irving. "Social Structure and Socialization for Change." Paper presented at Theory and Concept Development Workshop, Annual Meeting of the National Council on Family Relations, Portland, Oregon. November 1, 1972.

Yablonsky, Lewis. *Robopaths.* New York: Bobbs-Merrill, 1972, p. xiii.

# Chapter 4
# Family Members: Primary Influencers of Family Decisions

The family is a corporate unit. Its individual members are at some times interdependent, unable to function without the support of one another. At other times family members act independent of the family unit, yet influenced by the values that have been formed through family interaction.

Decision making in the family is a complex process. Its roots are in the genetic inheritance and psychological development of each member. It is shaped in part by the network of social exchanges that result in a family theme or value system. The interplay between individual needs and values, resulting in the value orientations underlying decision making, are discussed in this chapter.

Family members acting either in concert or individually are the primary determiners of family decisions. Because each family member has a unique genetic make-up and neural legacy, he or she perceives information and experiences in the environment in a particular and individual fashion. Individual needs and perceptions functioning largely below the level of consciousness generate different alternatives for family choice. To understand how the family detects those situations that require decisions, we must first understand how individuals perceive their environments, and how these perceptions are translated into images of reality. These images become the values, goals, and particular decisions and activities that families carry out. Some of the activities serve the individual, others are carried out for the family as a group. In the family, the activities of one member are interlocked with the activities of others; each member suffers or benefits from the activity of others.

The great majority of choices open to a family lie at the threshold of individual consciousness. Each family member perceives only a fraction of the alternatives open to the family. The perception of this fraction is the individual's first stage of choice. It is the beginning of "consciousness raising." Choice ultimately depends on individual perceptions of what exists; images of "what is possible." These perceptions depend on awareness and sensitivity to impressions. Both awareness and sensitivity to impressions are in some part shaped by neural inheritance as well as by past experiences. Each family member in one sense helps to create the environment to which the family organization responds.

Once the unconscious is raised to the level of awareness, certain possible alternatives come into focus for the decision maker. This second stage of choice, the conscious recognition of possible alternatives, sensitizes the decision maker to seeing the feasibility of alternatives, especially those that have particular interest and meaning to him or her. It is at this stage that values are brought from out of the unconscious to a level of awareness and consciousness.

From the range of alternatives that appear acceptable, interesting, and possible the decision maker begins to consider several possibilities. These possibilities are considered and screened on the basis of a particular purpose and for a particular situation and point in time. In this third stage goals come to the fore, and choice is more conscious and deliberate than previous stages. The decision maker is now in the position to select from among the alternatives generated. The last stage of the process is known as *decision making*, a deliberate and conscious act of selecting from between at least two alternatives or melding several alternatives into a course of action.

Clearly, a number of factors influence a final decision. Understanding what precedes the making of a decision is fundamental to understanding how decisions are made, for the individual styles of choice, the underlying individual values and goals, are all integral facets of family decisions (Hoyt, 1969).

## PERCEPTIONS

How individuals react to a situation is the result of the way they perceive that situation and also results from their particular behavioral dispositions at a point in time. Part of the reason why persons perceive things differently can be attributed to natural physiological differences; persons differ in their sensitivity to noise, smell, sight, touch, taste. The importance of these physiological differences becomes clear when observing persons who have limited capacity of one of the sense organs. Life is very different for these people, and the disability demands that they make very difficult adjustments.

Learning is another important factor in perceptual differences. A person whose early environment provided few stimuli had little opportunity to learn from a variety of experiences and to gain freedom in adjusting to new situations. Without opportunities for new perception, individuals show declining ability to solve problems. Their thinking becomes confused and disorganized, and they may become bored or unable to concentrate, or may even develop hallucinations. To function normally, humans must have regular contact with the outside world. The kind and number of stimuli available in the home environment are critical to the optimum development of children and, ultimately, to broadening the base for family decisions.

Personality factors contribute to the differences in individual perception. How individuals perceive the environment and how they perceive themselves are related. Behavior is highly influenced by whether people see themselves as adequate in a particular situation. Previous experiences of success and acceptance help develop a positive self-perception while rejection and failure contribute to negative self-perception. The way in which one perceives the environment may be considered as a perceptual defense, a means of protecting self-organization.

One's perception of the environment relates to how one perceives his or her body (Witkin et al., 1974). *Field independent* persons are highly sensitive to stimuli from their bodies, irrespective of outside environmental stimuli. They perceive themselves as highly differentiated from their environment and tend to remain independent of it. They are relatively unaffected by authority and are guided by their own values and needs. In contrast, *field dependent* persons are very sensitive to the outside environment and rely on others for guidance.

Whether one is "internally" or "externally" directed is critical to the stance one takes toward family decision making. Internally directed people perceive themselves as controlling the situation and have strong belief in their ability to improve conditions. Externally directed people believe fate has preordained what will happen, and that powerful "others" or environmental conditions control decision situations. Externals cannot predict the effect of behavior because the world is too complex and confusing (Rotter, 1971, p. 42); however studies indicate that people who are internally motivated believe they can control themselves and the environment (Rotter, 1971, p. 58). When associated with successful decision making, an internal orientation can lead to feelings of competence; when associated with failure, it can lead to self-blame. It is suggested that when internality involves excessive self-blame, it can be damaging to individuals, especially if they are members of minority groups affected by a faulty system or hostile environment.

Highly externally motivated people feel they are at the mercy of the environment. When they are manipulated, they take it in stride better than internally oriented persons. A focus on the external factors may be motivationally healthy if it results in assessing one's chances for success against real external obstacles.

The orientation of internality or externality is believed to be developed within the family setting early in life. A study of male adolescents indicates it may be related to the child's *perception* of parent-child decisions and relationship (Scheck et al, 1973, p. 651). The system of rewards and punishments used by parents help shape internal and external orientations.

## PERCEPTUAL ORGANIZATION

Perception is not the result of separate, distinct impressions, but of wholes. It is based on that part of a particular object or scene on which attention is focused while the remainder of the situation is relegated to the background of the perceptual field. Things, events, situations, become related one to another. Perception is organized through the patterning or grouping of stimuli so that the world is not perceived as a series of unrelated energy information changes. Certain stimulus characteristics influence the way in which what is perceived is patterned and organized. These characteristics are:

1. *Proximity*—objects that are close together are preceived as part of the same group.
2. *Stimulus similarity* — objects that resemble each other tend to be grouped together.
3. *Continuity* — stimuli that seem to form continuous patterns are perceived as wholes.
4. *Closure* — stimuli that seem to form part of a recognizable whole tend to be perceived together, as if the whole pattern were there.

Perception should help establish environmental stability. One way in which environmental stability is achieved is by perceiving the world as if it were fixed and stable. Common sense indicates that the earth is stable even though in reality it is spinning about the solar system. Another way of achieving stability is to perceive objects as having a constant shape, size, and color. For example, even though a table can be viewed from different angles, it is seen as having a fixed shape. When an adult is seen at a distance, he is still recognized as an adult rather than as a child. The constancy feature is a result of previous learning experiences.

Illusions, or perceptual inaccuracies, occur when an individual incorrectly interprets a particular set of stimuli. Any change in a familiar object requires new learning before accurate perception is possible. Sometimes misinformation is learned and accurate perception is impossible.

Many factors influence perception and indirectly influence the alternatives for choice. Among these are "mind set" and social pressure. There is a tendency to see in the environment what one wants or expects to see. The familiar or similar serves as a strong stimulus. The environment can be altered almost without awareness because of the "set" to perceive the familiar environment. Children are less likely to be deceived than adults because they have fewer expectations (fewer "sets") about the world. Hence, they can often be more creative in generating new alternatives. Much of the smooth functioning of everyday behavior can be attributed to the perception of certain familiar stimuli. Alternatives are readily known.

To check the accuracy of perceptions in the family, continuous searching for consensual validation or agreement of family members takes place. The fact that others agree does not mean that the perception is accurate. The need for validation leads to the assumption that family and other social pressures do in fact strongly influence individual perceptions. The individual can be unaware that the judgments of other people can predetermine or modify perceptions. Since perceptions form the basis of attitudes and actions, the individual may not be as independent in making decisions as he or she believes. As has been discussed, some individuals are more affected by external pressure than others.

How the individual internalizes stimuli and reacts to them is a factor in creating alternatives and opens the possibilities for selectively dealing with the environment. Compton and Hall (1972, pp. 21–22) summarize this process:

An individual masters his environment largely through the processes of differentiating-integrating, valuing-evaluating, and perceiving. Through the differentiation-integration process, the human being organizes the world into definable objects and people; then he refines the categories further. Valuing-evaluating includes the feeling tones accompanying experiencing. The individual sees himself as an entity and assigns values to himself, probably in relation to how he feels other people evaluate him on the basis of their actions toward him. Perceiving operates to aid in protecting the already achieved self-organization. Perceiving processes select what stimuli will be acted upon by the individual and screen out those that are out of tune with the present rhythm of the individual's self-development.*

Much of perception lies at the threshold of consciousness. At this level perceptions influence needs and values. This constitutes the beginning stage of choice making.

NEEDS

All persons have a complete set of needs which must be fulfilled at some level if the human is to survive. Like all living organisms, humans depend on the environment for resources to meet needs. For

*From *Foundations of Home Economics Research: A Human Ecological Approach* by Norma Compton and Olive Hall. Burgess Publishing Company, 1972.

example, humans cannot produce nutrients, they are dependent on the natural environment for resources to meet physical survival needs: nutrients, air, and water. And since humans are social organisms, they are equally dependent on other humans for that psychosocial development that gives meaning to their lives. Family membership provides one means for meeting these physical and social needs.

Maslow (1954, p. 80) holds that there is a hierarchical structure of needs that initiate goal-directed behavior. Before an individual is motivated to satisfy one of the higher motives, needs must be fulfilled at the levels that are below it in Maslow's hierarchy. These needs, in order are:

1. *Physiological needs.* Hunger, sex, and thirst are dominating needs. A person who lacks food, safety, love, and esteem would find the physiological demand for food his greatest need. The primitive-biological needs are homeostatic mechanisms maintaining body temperature at an optimal level, keeping a balance of minerals in the blood stream, and restoring the diseased or injured body to health. A person who has been deprived of physiological needs in the past reacts differently to present satisfactions than one who has never been deprived.

2. *Safety needs.* Next in the order of complexity are the needs related to maintenance of the physical self, a protection against the dangers of the environment. The need for safety may dictate a preference for familiar rather than unfamiliar things and for undisrupted routine or rhythm (a predictable, orderly world). Compulsive concern for safety may cause a person to try to order and stabilize the world so unexpected and unmanageable dangers will not appear.

3. *Belongingness and love needs.* When both physiological and safety needs are met fairly well, the individual experiences the need for a close, emotionally satisfying relationship with other persons. At first, the emphasis is on receiving, but love needs also involve giving. Effort is made to be a part of a group, such as family. There is a willingness to conform to group norms.

4. *Esteem needs.* These needs include a desire for self-respect, self-esteem, and the esteem of others. A person desires strength, achievement, adequacy, mastery, competence, independence,

status, recognition, attention, appreciation, dominance. When these needs are thwarted, an individual may develop feelings of inferiority, weakness, or discouragement. The person may compensate with neurotic behavior. Satisfaction of esteem needs builds self-confidence, strength, worth, and capability. Healthy self-esteem is based on deserved respect from others.

5. *Self-actualization needs.* Generally, these needs emerge after the first four levels are satisfied. Self-actualization refers to the realization of one's potential and ideals, the fulfillment of one's capabilities. A need for self-actualization may have "functional autonomy," being satisfying in itself regardless of the original need. An individual with a strong drive for self-expression may endure hunger, physical danger, and other forms of deprivation to satisfy this need.

These needs affect one's perception of the environment and influence family goal formation. All humans possess some degree of need for existence, relatedness, and growth (Alderfer, 1972).

*Existence needs* are individual requirements for material and information exchange to reach and maintain equilibrium. All forms of material and physiological desires are included: hunger, thirst, pay, fringe benefits, and physical working conditions. Beyond minimum needs, one person's gain can be another's loss, a point to keep in mind when attempting to examine the meeting of more than one individual's need in the family.

*Relatedness needs* are expressed in transactions with other persons: family members, coworkers, friends, enemies. Any group or individual can be a significant other if there is sustained interaction by choice or setting. Satisfaction of this need depends on mutual sharing and concern. A sense of distance or lack of connection is the opposite of relatedness satisfaction.

*Growth needs* emerge from going beyond the equilibrium state, interacting with and changing the environment, and increasing one's internal differentiation. A person or the family group is impelled toward productive and creative efforts that utilize abilities and may require the development of additional capacities. The environmental setting determines the extent to which there is opportunity to grow.

These existence, relatedness, growth needs are summarized in the table below.

| Need | Target | Process | Concreteness |
|------|--------|---------|--------------|
| Existence | Material substances | Getting enough | Most concrete |
| Relatedness | Significant others | Mutual sharing of thoughts and feelings | Concreteness varies: depends on consensual validation of two (or more) persons |
| Growth | Environmental settings | Joint processes of a person or family group becoming more differentiated and integrated as human beings | Least concrete: can be known only by family group or individual |

Alderfer (1972, p. 149) has identified a series of propositions, generated from empirical data, that relate needs to existence, relatedness, and growth. These propositions can be useful in identifying the relationship of needs to alternative goal formation in the family. To show how these might apply in family situations, one example is provided for each proposition.

**Proposition 1.** The less existence needs are satisfied, the more they will be desired.

Example: During the winter season there was a bad fire in the Miller's home. Once the fire was put out, the Miller's decision of highest priority was to find shelter for that night and until the house could be repaired.

**Proposition 2.** When both existence and relatedness needs are apparent, the less frequently relatedness needs are satisfied, the more existence needs will be desired.

Example: Jennie and Dave decided to try living together since both were having trouble getting along with their families. They rented a tiny cottage. Within a few months, they seemed to be in each other's way constantly when they were both home. Dave began spending a lot of time and money at a gambling casino. Jennie was unhappy about her relationship with Dave but she would have put up with the situation. However, when he began losing a lot of money and selling some of their furniture, she decided to take what she could and go back to her family. Her existence needs seemed more dominant as her relationship with Dave became worse.

**Proposition 4.** When relatedness needs are relatively dissatisfied, the less relatedness needs are satisfied, the more they will be desired. In addition when relatedness needs are relatively satisfied, the more relatedness needs are satisfied, the more they will be desired.

Example: Ken has very few friends and no friends of the opposite sex. He has a strong desire to date girls but can't seem to get any girl to go out with him. Ken's need for relatedness stems from his deprivation. On the other hand, Mark has several friends including a few girls he enjoys dating. The more he dates, the more he feels at ease with girls and the more dates he desires. Mark's need for relatedness grows out of satisfying experiences with others.

**Proposition 6.** When both relatedness and growth needs are relatively satisfied, the more relatedness needs are satisfied, the more growth needs will be desired.

Example: Sue and Pete have a beautiful relationship. Now that all of their children have left home, they have decided to pursue a long-standing interest. They are attending an adult education class in Spanish, and they are planning a trip to Mexico for their next vacation.

**Proposition 7.** When growth needs are relatively dissatisfied, the less growth needs are satisfied, the more they will be desired. When growth needs are relatively satisfied, the more growth needs are satisfied, the more they will be desired.

Example: Doris and Judy met at the community college where both are first-semester students. After raising her children to their teens, Doris felt her own growth had been stifled. She has a tremendous urge to get out into the world and earn some money just to prove that she could. She has no job skills and no idea what fields of work might be available to her if she had the training. Her desire for growth stems from a recognition of her previous lack of opportunities. In contrast, Judy has just moved to this community. She rushed over to the community college to see if they offered a child development curriculum. She had started this major at another college and enjoyed it so much that she wanted to continue her growth.

How needs are met depends on the ability of family members to perceive informational stimuli from the environment and the availability of matter-energy resources in the environment for carrying out essential family activities.

## VALUES

The particular values held by family members play an integral part in shaping family decision. Values come into play in all stages of the act of choice. They shape perceptions and influence the selection of goals as well as the perception and ranking of alternative means for reaching goals. Their particular role at the point of decision is twofold: (1) to serve as criteria for goal selection, and (2) to rank alternative goals in preferential order. Values are learned in the social milieu in which family members live. Hence, the family, in which the individual acquires primary learning, is critical in value formation. Valuing is a process that is learned from the natural, socioeconomic, and physiological environments in which one interacts. In turn, what a person values influences behavior and thereby affects the environment. According to Linton (1954, pp. 1, 45–68), a value is anything "capable of influencing the individual's decisions in choice situations, or, going one step back and as a necessary preliminary to such influence, anything capable of producing an emotional response." Values are learned beliefs that are internalized, they tend to arouse a strong emotional-intellectual response when something runs counter to them. Values are what we believe, transformed into feelings of what might be.

Values are concepts of the desirable. They are what one believes is right, good, or best, what one holds dear, prizes and cherishes, and feels a commitment toward. Values can be sources of guilt if particular actions are in conflict with the value. They seem to generate both commitment and self-inhibition. They impose feelings of obligation, helping individuals determine what they "ought to" do, how they "should" behave. They are what the individual strives for, that to which worth is attached. They are more than verbalizations, they become actions (Rescher, 1969, pp. 1–12).

Values represent an important link between the social environment and the individual's psychological being. "The usual form in which this linkage is stated posits values as mediating the effects of social structure on personality. That is, social location influences values, and values in turn influence psychological states of behavior" (Bengston and Lovejoy, 1973, p. 880). As conceptions of the desirable, values are ultimate and self-sustaining ends that can be rank-ordered or placed in priority. In this way, they serve as strong motivations of decision and action. Values are patterned beliefs that function at both the explicit (easily recognized and verbalized) or implicit (not easily recognized, subconscious, inferred from behaviors) level. They have an evaluative function; that is, they assist one in making judgments. Values are themselves alternatives implying usually some comparison between and among possible choices and actions (Rokeach, 1973, p. 73). Values seem to be related more to long-term, recurrent problems rather than fleeting and occasional short-range problems. They are characterized by continuity, commitment, and reinforcement. Seen thus, the value patterns of an individual are the criteria used in making the tough decisions concerned with allocating the scarce and limited resource of energy in all its forms throughout the life span.

Sources of Values

Values have deep-seated, often irrational origins in one's environment. A value system is built from all the forces, real and vicarious, to which a person is exposed—home, school, church, peers, the various subcultures to which one belongs as well as exposure to literature and mass media, especially television. The code of values a family exposes to its children affects their value formation. Parents who wish their child to value what they believe is "right" must first decide what they believe "ought to be."

From infancy, children are inculcated with their parents' values. Even though parents may not teach values deliberately, children sense what the parents consider to be good and bad. An inconsistent home environment is confusing to the children. They hear mother say never to lie, yet she tells a telephone caller that dad is not home when he is actually watching television. Dad approves a bicycle, but mother wants the son to wait another year. Who is right? How does a child sort out differences in the values of persons the child loves and respects? How does the child begin to develop ideas of what is desirable?

Children are quick to grasp whether or not they are loved. When parents show they care, their teaching by example is much more effective in inculcating values than when they teach by precept. Social values can be learned best by experience. Shannon (1972) has indicated that many parents are almost paralyzed by uncertainty. Many are not sure what their own values are. Others think they know but lack the confidence to impose discipline on behalf of their values. Shannon feels the worst situation results when parents doubt their right to structure a child's conduct and to influence the formation of values. A parent's indecision about values can have serious implications for the family and society. Decisions made in all areas of family life are outward expressions of the values the family holds. In keeping with their consciously determined values, the family selects goals and ways of pursuing them and, in this way, subtly or not so subtly, provides for value reinforcement. Thus the family shapes individual values, and through the actions of individuals environments are shaped.

### Value Classifications

A relatively simple way of classifying values is to sort them into three basic types: personal, moral, and social values.

1. *Personal values.* Character, or the manner in which an individual copes with everyday living, is expressed through such values as self-discipline, punctuality, respect for high-quality work, self-evaluation of one's effort and work, achievement, devotion to the task, decisiveness, orderliness, and goal orientation. These can be viewed as personal values. No one individual acts on all the values that might be considered desirable. What one person values differs from what another values.

Within a family, individuals have different values that affect their goal rankings as well as how they seek to implement their decisions. For example, Mrs. Lane may have high *theoretical* values (an interest in discovering the truth and relating one principle to another). After analyzing the family needs, she decides a food freezer would be desirable. Before she purchases any major appliance, she seeks facts on the design, operation, care, and use of a variety of models. Mr. Lane may have high *economic* values (a concern about the practical use of resources for meeting their material needs). He may value whatever serves to maintain and increase their quality of life, such as clean clothing, regular medical and dental services, and nutritional food, but not see how their limited resources can be extended to include a food freezer. Maria, their teen-age daughter, has high *aesthetic* values as shown in her talent of capturing and expressing the feeling and beauty of art forms. For her, the best use of the family's resources would include painting lessons. The range of values held by this family for the use of a limited monetary resource illustrates the need for a mediation of values among family members. It also illustrates that the act of choice is multivalued in most family situations.

2. *Moral values.* Rectitude, a sense of right and wrong, and responsibility to live in ways that protect the freedom and rights of others reflect one's concept of moral decency. Moral beliefs and attitudes are shown in honesty, dependability, tolerance, peace of mind, a sense of fair play, integrity, concern for long-range benefits, and consistency between one's ideals and actions. Values concerned with what is good and right behavior are classified as moral values.

3. *Social values.* In relationships with others, an individual shows such values as support, cooperation, recognition, independence, justice, benevolence, equity, conformity, respect for law, acceptance of majority rule, sense of interdependence, and a recognition of the worth and dignity of every human being.

The essence of moral and spiritual values is found in relating separate experiences to the total values of the individual's life, forming a unity of all one's experiences. A family with high religious values that are consistent with behavior will not only love a Supreme Being but will regard the development of satisfying human relationships within the family and outside the home as a major form of expressing this moral commitment. Likewise, in a family with high *social* values feelings of love and caring are revealed through their intimate sharing with each other. This permeates their relationships with other people, extending to their participation in community betterment.

Awareness of the needs of others and consideration for others are important to the development of values. Values are a crucial part of an individual's total development. They are the basis of commitments. They find expression in all areas of life: what kind of marriage partner one selects, how and where one chooses to live, how much risk and uncertainty each family member can tolerate, what kind of employment a person seeks and how one performs work, how individuals relate to other people, what they achieve, and how they find ways for self-expression and creativity, whether they see themselves as having mastery over the environment or living in harmony with it.

## Moral Imperatives

Moral development or conscience may influence the direction of desires as well as the intensity with which one seeks their fulfillment. A question such as the following can be approached from four different moral perspectives.

Should a pregnant 17-year-old unmarried girl have the baby or seek an abortion?

1. A *hedonistic* conscience would focus on the external consequences, fear rather than belief in the wrongness of an act, pleasure rather than belief in the rightness of an act. The girl's reasoning might be that she is already in trouble, so why take a chance on worse trouble. Having a child would ruin her life; an abortion would be in order.

2. An *authority-oriented* conscience would follow the rules or wishes of a religious, political, or parentally sanctioned authority. Fear of losing approval and status would be viewed as important. In handling this problem, the person might say that she was raised in a religious faith that condemned abortion and she should follow the sanction of her church.

3. The *other-directed* conscience would follow the dictates of a primary group even though that group may sanction deviant actions. The desire for love is so strong that the individual may give up her usual ethical standards in order to retain it. The girl may feel that she has followed her parents' advice all her life and should do so now. What she does will depend on her parents' concept of what is right.

4. An *integrity-oriented* conscience is highly internalized and is willing to violate the opinion of others or rules of authority in order to maintain individual integrity and social responsiveness, fearing

a loss of identity. One girl, acting from her inner source, might choose the abortion on the grounds that doing something that may not seem right to her may prevent ruining another life. Another girl may decide to have the baby, thinking that she made a mistake and now must pay for it.

Kohlberg (1973), relying heavily on Piaget's concept of human development, has examined moral development, especially in children. One can see how an individual's level of moral development is directly related to decision making. How free is a person who chooses to do something merely to avoid punishment? How congruent is the one who acts as a conformist, obeying laws and being good "so someone will love me"? Is an adult's behavior based on contractual-legalistic concerns or on a motivation to maintain self-integrity and respect for human dignity in interpersonal relations?

## Family Value Questions

Jacobson (1969, p. 1) posed some questions that can help families identify the values they hold. Family members can ask:

1. What is good and right behavior? These values—such as respect for life, for truth, for justice—are called moral values.
2. What is beautiful? That which brings pleasure, joy, or meaning into life because of its beauty is called an aesthetic value.
3. What is profitable? Those things that save money or make money represent economic values.
4. What is useful? Pragmatic values are reflected in those activities or articles that have utility.
5. What makes us feel good? Sensual values respond to the experiences, thoughts, and articles that meet needs for "feeling."
6. What is fashion? Prestige values are expressed through possessions and activities that have high status in society. Owning or doing the "in" thing reflects prestige values.
7. What is beyond man? Spiritual values are those expressed through religion and activities that portray meaning in an individual's life.

## Value Orientations

Individuals do not hold one, but rather a multiplicity of values. Through processes of everyday experiences in a variety of settings and the reaction of the person to these experiences, values are orchestrated into a pattern. Groups, as well as individuals, develop values in this way. These values orientations serve as guides to human behavior—to the choices and actions of both personal and family systems.

Value orientations are complex but definitely patterned (rank-ordered) principles resulting from the transactional interplay of three analytically distinguishable elements of the evaluative process—the cognitive, the affective, and the directive elements—which give order and direction to the overflowing stream of human acts and thoughts as these relate to the solution of "common human problems" (Kluckhohn and Strodtbeck, 1961, p. 4).

Problems common to all people and at all times seem to pivot around five critical questions. The questions that all human groups must deal with are: "What is the character of innate human nature? What is the relation of man to nature? What is the temporal focus of human life? What is the modality of human activity? What is the modality of man's relationship to other men?" (Kluckhohn and Strodtbeck, 1961). Each of these concerns are involved in the ways families make choices.

*Human Nature Orientation.* Persons can be viewed as evil, a mixture of good and evil, or good. The Puritan heritage conceives of humans as being basically evil, but perfectible through constant control and discipline of the self. In the United States today, the individual is generally viewed as a mixture of good and evil, whose lapses can be understood rather than severly condemned.

*Man-Nature Orientation.* A family's relationship to nature can be described as subjugation to nature, harmony with nature, or mastery over nature. Persons who feel that they are subject to nature generally accept what they believe to be the inevitable, feeling there is little they can do to control their destiny. Some groups view themselves in harmony with nature; that is, they see unity in man, nature, and supernature. The dominant orientation in highly technological societies is master-over-nature, a belief that natural forces are to be overcome and used by man. An emphasis on technology illustrates how humans have attempted to master nature, often at high costs to both man and nature. Recognition of the limits of the environment and its natural resources is causing humans to review their man-nature orientation.

*Time Orientation.* The meaning attached to time by various cultures can be thought of in terms of past, present, and future. Historical China and England, dominated by traditionalism, functioned from past orientation. Many Americans in the 1970s emphasized the present, paying little attention to the past and regarding the future as vague and unpredictable; an existential view seemed to prevail. Generally, highly educated and internally controlled groups emphasize the future and place high value on change as long as it does not threaten the existing order.

*Activity Orientation.* The three ways in which people express themselves through activity are being, being-in-becoming, and doing. Being is a spontaneous expression of human personality. There is concern for what the human being is rather than what he or she can accomplish. Being-in-becoming is concerned not only with what a person is, but how one is developing. The goal is that all aspects of the self are developed as an integrated whole with little competition or comparison of self with others. Doing demands the kinds of activity that result in accomplishments measurable by standards external to the individual; competition is acceptable and comparisons of success are common. Neurotically compulsive behavior and intense competition can arise from the doing emphasis.

*Relational Orientation.* In their relationship with other persons, humans function in a lineal, collateral, and individualistic manner. Lineal relations stress like-mindedness and behavioral similarities, while permitting leeway within the confines of fixed customs. Group goals and welfare are primary, continuity through family lines and traditions are paramount. Collateral relations stress that an individual is not a human being except as he or she is part of a social order. Individuals are biologically related to each other through time and have cultural continuity. The goals and welfare of the extended family (siblings and cousins) are primary. Dominant individualistic principles emphasize individual goals above collateral or lineal goals, yet the individual still has responsibility to the total society. The individual's place in society and his or her responsibilities are structured, independent of particular or collateral groups.

These value orientations, which function within a range of variability, underly the choices made in families. Families develop varying patterns of everyday living in order to meet the basic problems of human existence. Ways of coping with the physical environment are shaped by value orientations. In turn, the physical environment shapes values. In fact, the resources available in the environment are critical determinants of values.

Human values are dependent on the conditions of existence. Values change as conditions change, and, at the same time, conditions reflect value-based goals and their accompanying actions. Individuals, through actions that reflect values, seek an equilibrium with the conditions (environments) that surround them.

According to Graves (1970, pp. 133-134) values develop

from the existential states of man. These states emerge as man solves certain hierarchically ordered existential problems crucial to his existence. The solution of man's current problems of existence release free energy in his system and creates, in turn, new existential problems . . . . As each existential stage emerges, man believes that the problems of human existence are the problems with which he is faced at the level at which he has arrived. He develops, therefore, a general way of life . . . a thematic value system appropriate to his current existential state . . . his theme is specified into particular *schema for existence* as a result of individual, group and environmental differences.*

Different values seem to emerge at various levels of existence. Most environmental conditions allow existence at varying subsistence levels. When conditions are such that resources are very scarce, for example, if food and land are in extremely short supply, humans are motivated chiefly by physiological needs and no conscious value exists. Values are expressed in reactions to the environment. As conditions improve, motivations become less physiological, the motivational system is based on security or independence and values become materialistic. Under optimum conditions, experience becomes the motivator and values are those of communion—a harmony of humans with other humans and with nature. Changing values are inextricably tied to changing conditions. Family members move from value systems appropriate to restricted living circumstances to higher value systems appropriate to better conditions of life. As persons and their social systems develop, old values emerge into new values more appropriate to the new conditions.

*Clare W. Graves, "Levels of Existence: An Open System Theory of Values," *Journal of Humanistic Psychology*, Vol. 10 No. 2. Reprinted by permission.

## SUMMARY

Values are in constant process of emerging. As families grow and change, they change their environments. Over time the verbal, non-verbal, and autistic systems of human communication, particular customs, and different ways of organizing family life have emerged, based on the variations in human values. These patterned and hierarchically arranged value systems underlie the transactional processes that occur between individual family members and the family unit as well as the natural and human-built environment that surrounds them. Out of this valuing process comes specific family goals. It is this basic valuing process that guides choice making and through the decisions made, and actions taken, shapes the future of humanity.

## SELECTED REFERENCES

Alderfer, Clayton P. *Existence, Relatedness, and Growth.* New York: The Free Press, 1972.

Bengston, Vern L., and Mary Christine Lovejoy. "Values, Personality and Social Structure." *American Behavioral Scientist.* 16, 6 (July/August 1973): 880-912.

Compton, Norma H., and Olive A. Hall. *Foundations of Home Economics Research: A Human Ecology Approach.* Minneapolis: Burgess Publishing Company, 1972.

Graves, Clare W. "Levels of Existence: An Open System Theory of Values." *Journal of Humanistic Psychology.* 10, 2 (Fall 1970): 131-134.

Hoyt, Elizabeth E. *Choice and the Destiny of Nations.* New York: Philosophical Library, Inc., 1969.

Jacobson, Margaret. *Values I.* East Lansing, Mich., Michigan Cooperative Extension Service, Extension Bulletin E-647. April 1969, p. 1.

Kluckhohn, Florence R., and Fred L. Strodtbeck. *Variations in Value Orientations.* Evanston, Ill.: Row, Peterson and Co., 1961.

Kohlberg, L., and E. Turil (Eds.). *Recent Research in Moral Development.* New York: Holt, Rinehart and Winston, 1973.

Linton, Ralph. "The Problem of Universal Values." In *Methods and Perspectives in Anthropology.* Robert F. Spencer (Ed.). Minneapolis: The University of Minnesota, 1954, pp. 145-168.

Maslow, Abraham H. *Motivation and Personality.* New York: Harper, 1954.

Piaget, J. *The Moral Judgment of the Child.* New York: The Free Press, 1965.

Rescher, Nicholas. *Introduction to Value Theory.* Englewood Cliffs, N.J.: Prentice-Hall, 1969.

Rokeach, Milton. *The Nature of Human Values.* New York: The Free Press, 1973, p. 73.

Rotter, Julian B. "External Control and Internal Control." *Psychology Today.* 4 (June 1971): 37-42, 58-59.

Scheck, Dennis C., Robert Emerick, and Mohammed M. El-Assal. "Adolescents' Perception of Parent-Child Relations and the Development of Internal-External Control Orientation." *Journal of Marriage and the Family.* 35, 4 (November 1973): 643-655.

Shannon, William V. "What Code of Values Can We Teach Our Children?" *New York Times Magazine.* January 16, 1972.

Witkin, H., R. B. Dyk, H. F. Fatkvson, D. L. Goodenough, S. A. Karp. *Psychological Differentiation.* New York: Halstead Press Division, John Wiley & Sons, Inc., 1974.

# Chapter 5
## Family Organization: Determinant of Family Decisions

Family members organize themselves into a system for making decisions about the use of resources. In large measure these resources determine the structure and function of the family. Family role patterns, how they are formed and enacted, are the result of interactions over time of family members and environments. These role patterns determine the content and process of family decisions.

Because each family member is an individual, the family organization must serve as an adaptation system and assist family members as they confront one another and mediate actions among themselves and with the environment. This adaptation takes place in everyday living through the interaction and response (feedback) of persons to persons and persons to things. Families both adapt to and concurrently influence the natural environment and the development, structure, and activities of the human-built environments. The relationships that occur at the interface of family members and the environment helps define both the function and form of the family system. In turn, the particular functions the family unit carries out and the form the family takes influence its adaptive capabilities, such as the

74

ways in which it processes energy (both information and matter) so that essential needs are met and selected values mediated. The decisions families make about how resources will be used determine the quality of living the family will attain and the viability of the environments which surround the family.

## FAMILY FUNCTIONS

The functions of the family are reflected in the patterns of relationships among people and between people and environment. These functions can be thought of as sets of everyday activities essential to the survival and enhancement of the family group. These functions include procreation, the bearing of children; socialization, caring for and educating family members to function in the family and other social systems; and economic concerns, transforming energy-matter into activities that are useful to family members or to the larger society.

William Frankena (1970, pp. 10-14) has delineated a normative set of family functions; that is, a value-based set of functions that the family ought to carry out. These functions are: (1) making the lives of individual members as good as possible and, at the same time, dissuading the individuals from seeking their own good at the expense of others; (2) transmitting patterns of living and valuing from generation to generation (this is primarily an *educative* function); (3) regulating behavior in both a moral and social sense through discipline based on education rather than restraint; (4) assisting with the achievement of identity or self-definition for each member; (5) providing a center of leisure for the pursuit of goals that are aesthetic rather than material as a means for countering alienation and sense of powerlessness of members; (6) providing a seat of love and emotional gratification; and (7) helping to build for each member a way of thinking about life and the world, a view of humans and the universe.

Family functions were identified by the 1970 White House Conference on Children as a set of tasks to be accomplished. The study concluded that "the primary tasks of families are to develop their capacities to socialize children, to enhance the competence of their members to cope with the demands of other organizations in which they must function, to utilize these organizations, and to provide the satisfactions and a mentally healthy environment intrinsic to the well-being of a family" (Report of *Forum 14*, 1970, p. 228).

These functions are qualitative in nature. They assume that sustenance in the form of food and protection for physiological survival are essential. The basic physiological needs and accompanying functions provide the motivation and framework for decision making and managing in the family: values translated into goals; goals carried to action through the use of resources. In short matter-energy is transformed into information, goods, and services.

## ROLES OF FAMILY MEMBERS

Functions are reflected in the roles family members assume; for example, parent, wife, husband, son, daughter, employed worker. To put it simply, a role is doing what one is expected to do. Role information includes what is to do what, when, and how often, as well as what kinds of attitudes each is to maintain toward the other and the environment. In the family, information of this kind helps define the obligations and rights of each family member and of the family as a unit. At one level, these rights become rules or guides for making decisions about interpersonal and family behavior.

Many myths have arisen regarding roles that family members play or should play. Taking a role implies a relationship with someone else, for instance, the role of mother assumes the existence of someone who is to be mothered. A role assigns behavior to certain positions in relationship with the significant others. Roles in the family are both affective and instrumental; that is, they define feelings as well as actions. They are in some measure ascribed by both physiology and the culture (i.e., one is born a brother or sister). At the same time roles are achieved by interaction with others in a variety of environments. Family roles are particular rather than universal, that is, one is a particular person's wife or parent, rather than everyone's wife or mother. Family roles are diffuse rather than specific. Roles provide a method of organizing expectations and determining rules for acting. The family organization orders statuses, roles and the relations that hold them together.

When particular patterns or roles have fairly consistent consequences that give support to the culturally established way of life in a society, they are called *social functions*. The functions that involve recognized needs and gratifications to individuals create bonds between family members. Those functions recognized as valuable or essential to the welfare of society—care and education of children, for example—are implemented by societal regulation of family affairs (Turner, 1970, p. 217).

### Role Expectations

A role expectation can be described as what others expect you to do or the behavior you expect from others. Roles are the sets of norms or expectations held by anyone (usually significant others) for the behavior of a person in a particular position, such as what parents expect of children or husbands of wives. When these expectations stem from social sources such as friends, colleagues, or persons in authority, they are called norms. Expectations are concepts, standards, or anticipations of the behavior that is likely to be exhibited by a person.

In most family situations one person knows more than another about what behavior and attitudes are appropriate. For example, parents may have a more intricate cognitive map of a situation than their children have. Role teaching, whether done consciously or unconsciously, is an important part of the socialization process. Each person in a social encounter is simultaneously a teacher and a student in the reciprocal interaction process—a parent learns from a child while the child is learning from the parent.

Role expectations differ from person to person and family to family. Some expectations stem from social agreement. Some are culturally ascribed patterns of behavior. Normative standards may differ from the individual's role concept—what the person considers to be appropriate behavior in a particular situation. The role concept may differ from actual behavior. Role acceptance, then, depends on whether one is pleased to do what is expected, is indifferent, or is resentful.

### Role Conflict

An individual may experience role conflict when prescriptions or standards (criteria for behavior) one holds for oneself or those held for the person by others are inconsistent. Such conflict may result if the role definers disagree about the content of the behavior. For instance, the father is willing that the son have a motorcycle but the mother is afraid he may hurt himself. Sometimes the conflict is internal, as when the parents agree on their expectations but the child cannot fulfill all of the obligations simultaneously because some are contradictory or mutually exclusive. For example, the parents agreed that Mary could have a long dress if she earned the money and made her own dress. The day before she was to wear the dress, she had a chance to earn money assisting a friend's family with a dinner party. If she accepted this job, she would not have time to complete her dress. Some conflicts arise from the multiplicity of roles an individual assumes, such as when a homemaker wants very much to participate in a growth group that meets at the same time she must serve as a volunteer at the school library.

Rapidly changing roles in today's society increase the possibility of role conflict. Women who were once confined to being daughter, wife, and mother may also find themselves as breadwinner, professional, or politician. Easen (1961, pp. 24-28) summarized some of the conflicting demands in the roles of middle-class family members that existed in America in the early 1960s. He stated that:

> The *man* had almost overwhelming responsibility for the material welfare of his wife and children. Other members of the family often had little or no understanding of his occupational life. As a result of his high focus on his work life, his sharing of activities and family companionship typically fell below optimum. He was made to feel guilty about not serving as "leader, guide, business head, source of hand-outs, supervisor of work and recreation, arbiter, moral authority and character builder." His wife may have resented his not fitting the image. As a father, he was reduced to an "occasional, often unpredictable and violent, disapproval of the child"—which was intended to reinforce the mother's discipline.
>
> The *woman* had been conditioned in school to be individualistic and competitive. Upon marriage, she was expected to put the interests of her family above her individual interests. The diffuseness of her activities did not provide a sense of achievement that could come from focusing on a few central tasks. Affairs of lesser significance to the community were left for her while men took care of the more basic affairs. Although she found growing acceptance in careers, she felt blamed for delinquency, psycho-

logical disturbance or divorce that occurred in the family of the working mother. She wanted to be a "good mother" and yet she was fraught with anxiety about what it meant and how to become one. As a mother she must love and care for children but, when the father was away, she served as disciplinarian and character-molder. When her children became independent and self-sufficient, she found she was no longer familiar or comfortable with other useful roles. She was expected to remain attractive and interesting while facing the household chaos. She could keep well-informed and interesting by participating in civic affairs, but her husband may have resented her absence from home and neglect of duties. . . .

The *child* grew up in an environment in which his needs were satisfied by a very few persons. Dependency and psychological identification were heavily weighted toward the mother. The male child might find such feminine identification built psychological processes that were difficult to integrate later with the initiative and aggressiveness demanded of the male. He was trained to be peaceful and cooperative, yet to stand up for himself and be assertive. The adolescent clung to personally indispensable services (an allowance, use of the family car) while seeking to escape the controls of those providing the services. Parents fought to keep control in matters important to them. The adolescent "fluctuated between extreme dependence and defiant independence, gyrating from idealism to cynicism, from lush romancing to raw sexual aims, from fawning conformity to unyielding non-conformity."

Although role expectations of particular family members have changed somewhat in content over time, some basic roles of men and women have remained relatively consistent; most men continue to assume the paid employment role and many women, the nurturing role. Women are assuming paid employment in increasing numbers. On a worldwide basis, however, the gainfully employed role for women is secondary (Blake, 1974, p. 137). The major sexual revolution of the mid-seventies is identified by increasingly complex environments that have changed family roles and directly affected decision making. Carlfred Broderick (1976, p. 17) has reflected that: "If more mothers are entering the labor market, we must assume that some mothers have weighed the alternatives and have decided to go to work instead of staying home." This decision directly affects the role of all family members, for changes in female roles necessitate accompanying changes in male roles.

The environment thus becomes a part of shaping roles. One way of viewing this change is to see roles as expanding or being enlarged. Narrow, traditional, stereotyped definitions of sex roles disappear. Men become freer to express themselves in behaviors that were once considered feminine, and women's options expand to include behaviors that were considered unfeminine.

One complication of the enlarged options is the fragmentation of roles. For example, a woman can be thought of as a wife, mother, homemaker, paid worker, or career professional. Also, she can be seen as citizen, humanitarian, transmitter of the culture, and participator in social and recreational activities. Her role as a homemaker might be subdivided into such tasks as nursemaid, dietitian, food buyer, cook, dishwasher, housekeeper, laundress, seamstress, practical nurse, maintenance woman, gardener, and chauffeur in addition to the many roles that lend emotional support and inspiration to the family. Her roles are many and fragmented. But she is first of all a totality, a unique entity, a person who has potential for growth, regardless of the number of roles assumed.

Family members respond to the changing environments by changing both their role expectation and role performance. They respond to environmental demands by changing their internal ordering of activities and division of labor. These changes, brought about by family member-environmental interaction, helps identify the kind of decisions families will make.

## FAMILY FORMS

Families differ in their adaptive capacities largely because of their form: the configuration of age, sex, martial status, and role pattern of family members. Families vary in form over time and across cultures. Variant family forms have been identified and studied by M. B. Sussman (see Table 1, p. 81), who observes that "mapping of this pluralism in family structure indicated the beginnings of vast and cataclysmic changes in societal institutions and values, with obvious consequences for the traditional family" (1976, p. 14). Variation in family structure implies that there are several optimal ways of living,

Table 1
Variant Family Forms

| Family Type | | Estimated % Distribution | |
|---|---|---|---|
| Nuclear family | Husband, wife and offspring living in a common household, first marriage. | 45 | |
| | a. Single career | | 30 |
| | b. Dual career | | 15 |
| Nuclear family | Husband, wife and offspring living in a common household, remarried. | 10 | |
| Nuclear Dyad | Husband and wife alone: childless, or no children living at home. | 15 | |
| | a. Single career | | 4 |
| | b. Dual career | | 11 |
| Nuclear Dyad | Husband and wife alone: childless, or no children living at home, remarried | 5 | |
| Single-parent family | One head, as a consequence of divorce. abandonment or separation (with financial aid rarely coming from the second parent), and usually including preschool and/or school-age children. | 15 | |
| | a. Career | | 11 |
| | b. Noncareer | | 4 |
| Three-genera-tion family | May characterize any variant of family forms above living in a common household. | 2 | |
| Kin network | Nuclear households or unmarried members living in geographical proximity, operating within a reciprocal system | 2 | |
| Emerging experimental | a. Commune family | 6 | |
| | b. Unmarried parent and child family —usually mother and child, where marriage is not desired or possible. | | |
| | c. Unmarried couple and child family —usually a common-law marriage. | | |
| | d. Intentional couples | | |

Adapted from M. B. Sussman, "Toward Parity in Family Roles." *Penney's Forum: New Perspectives on Changing Roles.* Spring/Summer 1976. New York: J. C. Penney Company, page 14.

and that one can choose to pursue a lifestyle and family form that will bring about the greatest self-actualization. The fact that environments are becoming increasingly complex seems to indicate that the multiplicity of roles will continue and may, in fact, increase in the future. The movement toward equality or parity roles brings concurrent opportunities and freedom to *decide* what family form will provide the best nurturing environment for family members. Implicit also in variant structures is the opportunity and freedom to *decide* what roles will be played within that family structure.

Each of these family forms respond differently to its environment, and hence makes different choices. Through continuous system-environmental interaction over time, family members and the family unit grow, change, and develop. The following vignettes illustrate variant family forms and stages of development.

Betty, 25, has been married four years to Larry, also 25. She worked as a secretary while Larry completed his baccalaureate degree and law school. Within a few months of his passing the bar examination and finding a position in a law office they had their first baby. Betty quit her job and is devoting all her energies to being a homemaker. She enjoys cooking, looking after the baby, and engaging in creative activity as she finds time. Larry's law practice keeps him very busy, and he recently became involved in a political campaign. When he is home, he enjoys feeding and cuddling the baby. Larry and Betty are managing to make insurance payments for future security, as well as to put small amounts into a savings account to provide for their son's development and future education.

Sam and Mary Ellen were married four years ago, also. Sam is 45 and brought 4 children from his first marriage to this new family. Mary Ellen is 42, with two children from a first marriage. Sam is a successful businessman. Mary Ellen has never worked outside her home. Both Sam and Mary Ellen have found the adjustments to their new family more difficult than they expected. Mary Ellen likes a neat house, and four additional children who weren't trained to put things away upset her routine. Sam has difficulty relating to Mary Ellen's children, and both of them are upset by adjustment problems between the children. Mary Ellen's first husband always kept things peaceful at home; Sam is often on long trips and likes to rest when he is at home. He expects Mary Ellen to take care of all disciplinary problems with the children. Recently, Mary Ellen has been thinking about looking for a job, so she would have a few hours away from home each day—six teen-agers are quite a few in the house at one time.

Charles and Dorothy are both 28 years old. They have no children, and are each on the threshold of promising careers. Charles is a designer and Dorothy is in merchandising. They live in a new condominium for adults, which has an extensive clubhouse and athletic facilities. Their work schedules are demanding and erratic. At peak load times, Charles may work weeks nearly around the clock to complete a project. But when he has several weeks with a very light schedule, he is most unhappy with Dorothy's work schedule of several nights and Saturdays at the store. Neither of them likes to do housework, so the dishes stack up in the sink. They find themselves going out to eat just to avoid the mess in the kitchen. Charles complains about the amount of money Dorothy spends on clothes, which she feels she needs for her work. They have recently shifted to having Dorothy pay the bills and keep the financial records, because Charles really didn't like that chore.

Jean, 48, and Jim, 52, are both professors at the University. Their children are grown and live in other cities. Jean didn't work when the children were small. Now the house is empty and she is glad she has a career. She enjoys the interaction with students. She and Jim have found their relationship much closer since they share intellectual interests, work schedules, and many common problems. Jean always did everything in the house when she was at home, now Jim always fixes lunches and sometimes supper, when Jean is tired. They find they eat out a lot with friends who have similar interests. Jean has started doing more work in the yard. That used to be Jim's job, but she finds it relaxing after a day on the campus.

Gloria, 36, and Tom, 45, have been married just three years. It is the second marriage for each. Gloria had no children, Tom has three who are grown and rarely visit, although they do write occasionally. When they met, Gloria was a secretary in the company where Tom is an accountant. Now she works for a different firm. Gloria finds this marriage very different from her first unhappy experience. Tom supports her interest in becoming an executive with the company; his support has given her a lot of self-confidence. His pride in her accomplishments has encouraged her to take on assignments she would have been afraid of before. While Tom is always willing to fix a meal for himself if Gloria has to work late, she really likes to cook his favorite foods and often entertains friends from his office at buffet dinners. She has learned to enjoy Tom's willingness to do the laundry and take responsibility for the care of their cars, which she never enjoyed when she lived alone.

Lisa is 33 and has the sole responsibility for Bob, 12, and Johnny, 8. She has been divorced five years, and has received only sporadic child support from John, the boys' father, who lives in another state. Lisa and John were married when she was a sophomore in college, and she dropped out of school when Bob was born. She has occasionally worked as a waitress or cleaning woman in motels. Her health is not good, so she is unable to keep a job and is dependent on Aid for Dependent Children, food stamps, and occasional money from the boys' grandparents for income to pay the rent and buy food, Recently she decided to move back to the college town where she lived before she married and try to complete her degree. She is very uneasy about her abilities as a student, but she sees this as a possible escape from the financial bind she is continually in.

Marie is 22, with four children under six. She has never lived with the father of any of them longer than about six months. She receives Aid to Dependent Children and welfare support. Sometimes she is able to find work for a few weeks, and her younger sister or her grandmother takes care of the children. She tries to keep her little apartment neat and pretty. She has recently become involved with a community action group in her neighborhood, which is pressuring the city to clean up a vacant block and provide a park for the children. Through this group she has learned about classes in nutrition education and skill training, and she plans to become involved in them when the baby gets older. Right now she enjoys her children and is trying to bring them up to be healthy and happy.

Ann is 28 and has been divorced for six years. She has two children, Mary who is 8 and Sally who is 5. Ann is a teacher and works at the local high school. Her husband has never provided financial support for the children since their divorce. Ann has found her work schedule a good one, for she has vacations when the children do. She has considerable administrative ability, but has refused offers for advancement in this area since it would mean she wouldn't have as much time with the girls. The biggest problem she has had is finding someone to care for her children when they are sick or when she has to go to a conference. Doctors and dentists don't arrange their schedules for working mothers! When the girls were small, they lived in a small apartment. Recently, Ann made a down payment on a house. Now she is busy painting, papering, and learning elementary carpentry skills. She is enjoying a course in landscape architecture one evening a week and looking forward to planting flowers and building a patio in the spring.

Tom, 24, Betty, 22, Randy, 26, Steve, 25, Sue, 25, and Bill, 22, live together in a large old house in the heart of a small city in the Midwest. They have lived there for three years. Betty does all the cooking for the family, as well as food purchasing and a little sewing and clothing repair. The others all have at least part-time jobs and contribute a portion of their income to cover rent, utilities, and food. There are three children in the family, ranging in age from 3 to 5 years old. The members of the family arrange for their care according to their work schedules. Often the men in the family are home during the day and take care of the children. The children are familiar with contemporary music and enjoy singing and dancing. They have lots of grown-up friends who stop by to visit members of the family. No one really likes to clean, so the family has agreed that the first Saturday of every month will be cleaning day, and they all work together to get it done.

Don, a 29-year-old travel agent, is the father of three boys. He has never been married and adopted the first boy, Tommy, about four years ago. This last year Don and Tommy decided to expand their family, and now two other boys have been adopted. Don has found it relatively easy to take care of the boys, since they were school age when he adopted them. Don's schedule is flexible enough to allow him to be at home when he is needed; for illness, for instance. It also allows him to take the boys on extended weekend camping trips when they have a free school day. Don is teaching the boys to take care of their own rooms, and they are learning to do the laundry. Tommy is able to cook simple suppers, and Jim and Bill will learn soon. Don's parents enjoy their new grandchildren, and Don's sister has been able to stay with the children when Don has had to travel.

Donna and her baby girl, Marie, live in a tiny apartment in a small city. Donna is 18. Marie was born this last year when Donna was finishing high school. Marie's father, Dave, was Donna's boy friend in high school, but they decided not to get married, and he has moved to another city. Donna's parents tried to force the marriage and then refused to see her when she did not marry. They feel she disgraced them. Donna was a stenographic major in high school, but is unable to find a way to leave the baby and work, although she is an excellent typist. She loves Marie very much and takes good care of her. Donna finds she is very lonely; she doesn't have much in common with her girlfriends from high school now. She used some money Dave gave her when the baby was born to buy a TV and she watches it all day. Aid to Dependent Children is all the income Donna has. She has to budget very carefully for it to last all month.

Kay, 47, and Polly, 53, are both professional women with responsible positions in their companies. They met in the professional women's service organization in their city. Recently they purchased a home together. They opened a joint bank account to handle housing and living expenses, in addition to their separate personal accounts. They are enjoying the additional space and the large yard. Polly likes to work outside and has trimmed the trees and poured a new cement sidewalk. Kay refinishes furniture and has space for a workshop, and for the finished products. Both of them find they enjoy the secure feeling of someone else in the house after years alone. They are looking forward to retirement when they can become involved in the neighborhood and in many creative projects they don't have time for now.

Each family structure and role pattern creates a different setting for decision making, generates different alternatives for person-to-person and person-environment adaptations. The vignettes illustrate variant forms pursuing similar functions. An examination of the structure, role pattern, and essential functions inherent in each family vignette should be helpful in determining the "rules" the family organization uses to manage family-environment interactions and outcomes. Knowledge of these factors is helpful in predicting the kind of decisions each family will make, where the decisions will be made and implemented, who in the family will have the authority to decide, who will carry them out, and who will bear the responsibility and the consequences of the choice.

## FAMILY-ENVIRONMENT COSTS AND BENEFITS

The family organization is, in essence, a resource (matter-energy and information) exchange network: a group of persons who exchange information through interaction and communication and make decisions about the use of resources. The natural environment is the source of resources: energy in the form of information and matter. The family organization controls these energy flows through the decisions it makes. Any organization is, by nature, a system that will continously reorder people and resources if they become disordered in the course of interaction and resultant change. The family organization is in the continuous process of ordering and transforming energy into useful purposes for the family ecosystem. This processing is its major activity.

Energy enters the family in two major ways: (1) through the incorporation of a wide variety of informational stimuli about goods, services, and relationships over which the family organization has a measure of control and (2) through the ingestion of nutrients by family members. Adams (1975, p. 5) suggests that energy passes from environments to families and back to the environment through the family members who carry out activities in their different statuses and roles as well as through the institutionalized ways families receive benefits from the social environment.

Any transformation of energy between families and environments has a cost as well as a benefit to both. It takes energy to utilize energy. One way to view the energy costs, as well as the benefits or outcomes of family-environment interaction, is to identify the essential tasks of the family organization. These tasks are: (1) self-maintenance, (2) substenance-producing activities, (3) interaction with essential external groups, and (4) creative activities. Each of these tasks uses energy; yet each is essential to the family ecosystem. The amount of energy available and utilized will determine the level and standard of living possible for the family and the ability of the environment to sustain that level and standard.

### Self-Maintenance

Every organization uses energy merely to maintain itself. The family organization uses energy in maintaining family members in interlocking activities and in forming individual members into a corporate, interdependent group. The minimal energy expenditure needed to maintain the family as a unit is not known at this time, but it seems reasonable to anticipate that a figure could be computed by determining both time spent in interaction among family members and the physiological (caloric) costs of the interactions.

### Substanance-Producing Activities

Every organization expends energy to carry out those substantive functions for which it was designed. The family is organized to fulfill those functions that an individual cannot effectively carry out alone. These functions, as identified earlier, center around procreation, socialization, caring and nurturing of members, and working inside and outside the family in order to acquire and transform resources. The energy required for carrying out each of these activities can be computed by determining each family member's physiological energy costs (calories) as well as the energy costs of matter used. This would include costs of converting fossil fuels (matter) into electricity, gasoline, and other sources of power.

### Intergroup Interaction

Energy is expended by members of the family organization in creating and carrying out relations with individuals and groups external to the family. These would include interactions with neighbors, friends, coworkers, classmates, social agencies, and government. One way to compute these costs would be to determine the number of these activities and the amount of time they take. Again energy costs could be determined by caloric and material costs.

### Creative Activities

Energy is expended in what appears to be "doing nothing"—in thinking and feeling. This energy, which is comprised primarily of the cognitive activity of processing information—the unseen act of making decisions—is the creative function of the family organization. The family decision makers need energy, measured in time, to generate creative adaptations either of the internal functioning of the family organization or of the environments in which the family is embedded.

When energy is limited, it is expended first in maintaining the family unit and in carrying out those functions essential to the mere survival of individual members. Surplus or added energy is necessary for relating to increasingly numerous and diverse environments and for generating creative family-environmental relationships.

### SUMMARY

The family organization is, in essence, a resource exchange network. The natural environment is the basic source of resources: energy in form of information and matter. Families make decisions about the use of these resources. Making decisions and taking actions to transform energy into useful forms consumes energy. The costs and benefits to families and environments can be understood by assessing energy needed to maintain the family as a corporate unit, sustain the life of each family member, allow family and members to interact with social systems external to the family, and for discovery, experimentation, and creation of new adaptations. The major task of the family organization is to prudently manage energy so that all families can exist beyond the level of mere human survival.

## SELECTED REFERENCES

Adams, Richard N. *Energy and Structure, A Theory of Social Power.* Austin: University of Texas Press, 1975.

Blake, Judith. "The Changing Status of Women in Developed Countries." *Scientific American.* 231 (September 1974): 137-147.

Broderick, Carlfred B. "Roles, Family and Change." *Penney's Forum: New Perspective on Changing Roles.* Spring/Summer, 1975. New York: J. C. Penney Company. p. 17.

Eason, Elmer. "Problems and Strains in Middle-Class Family Life." *California Journal for Instructional Improvement.* 4 (October 1961): 24-28.

Frankena, William. "Toward a Philosophy of the Family." Paper presented at the Clara Brown Arny Symposium on Family Values, School of Home Economics, University of Minnesota, Minneapolis, Minn. March 1970, pp. 10-14.

Sussman, M. B. et al. "Changing Families in a Changing Society." *Forum 14 in Report to the President: White House Conference on Children.* Washington; U.S. Government Printing Office, 1970, p. 228.

Sussman, M. B. (Issue Editor). "Variant Marriage Styles and Family Forms." *The Family Coordinator.* 21, 4 (October 1974).

Sussman, M. B. (Issue Editor). The Second Experience: Variant Family Forms and Life Styles. *The Family Coordinator.* 24, 4 (October 1975).

Sussman, M. B. "Toward Parity in Family Roles." *Penney's Forum: New Perspectives on Changing Roles.* Spring/Summer, 1976. New York: J. C. Penney Company.

Turner, Ralph H. *Family Interaction.* New York: John Wiley & Sons, 1970, p. 217.

# Part Two
## Processes of Adaptation in the Family

# Chapter 6
## Decision Making in the Family Ecosystem

The process of making decisions and acting on them links families and environments. Through this continuous process information and materials are transformed and both families and environments change over time. This chapter examines social, economic, and technical decision making and their interrelatedness.

Decision making is the central activity of the family organization. It encompasses both unconscious and conscious behavior of family members as they act and react to the great body of potentials available in their environments. From this large perceptual set *particular* alternatives are *detected* by the family decision maker(s) and brought to the level of awareness and consciousness. It is from this specific set of alternatives, generated in response to specific demands, that decisions are made; alternatives are *selected or resolved* and actions *effectuated* (Hoyt, 1969, pp. 6-15; Kuhn, 1974, pp. 41-44). In essence, decision making involves: (1) the recognition of need for decision, (2) identifying and weighing acceptable alternatives, and (3) selecting or mediating an alternative and facilitating its action.

## DECISION MAKING AS PROCESS

Decision making is a process of reducing dissonance between the family and its environment as well as between and among family members. It begins with a desire for change, feelings of discomfort, doubt, unpleasantness, or uncertainty (i.e., reality differs from what is desirable or desired). It terminates in a commitment to one alternative that has either been selected from among acceptable alternatives or determined by melding different alternatives so that a new one emerges. The process is dynamic but exhibits continuity of time and interest. The continuity is evinced by the flow of thoughts, ideas, facts, and feelings (information) over time. *The process has movement.*

The movement, however, is not random. Information is ordered. It is in relating one feeling with another, a present idea with one from the past, an action with a given condition so that structure is given to the process. Thus, values, events, feelings, facts, and observations become ordered and integrated, demands are recognized, alternatives detected.

Integration alone, however, does not result in a decision. After ordering, discrimination must occur. Without discrimination, indecision remains. The decision maker(s) must be able to discriminate between what is important and what is not, between what is relevant and what is irrelevant, between actions that will achieve objectives and those that will not. Alternatives are weighed and closure is reached: a choice is made.

### Decision-Making Style

Decision making involves processing information from the environment by the decision maker(s). Decision makers process information in different ways. Bustrillos has defined decision-making style as the way in which decision makers pattern behavior. The pattern is disclosed as the decision maker's creative product of detecting demands from the environment and blending them with the needs and desires of the decision maker (Bustrillos, 1963, p. 5).

Elements of decision-making style are: mode, time reference, and decision-making rule, all of which are components of the process just described.

*Mode* is a way of developing ideas. In the process of deciding, inputs . . . are needed. These inputs, interpreted broadly, are information related to the decision-making problem. It shows how ideas are developed, analyzed, classified and then related to the decision-making problem (Bustrillos, 1963, p. 6).

Modes can be hypothetical, factual, or action-suggestive. When ideas are stated conditionally, conjecturally, or doubtfully, the mode is hypothetical. Statements such as "either-or," "maybe," or "perhaps" are used.

When ideas about things observed, sensed or apprehended are stated unconditionally, definitely, or conclusively, the statement is factual. The statement is verified, stated as belief or opinion, expressed as an attitude or compared with known things.

When action is directly suggested, the mode is action-suggestive. Statements prescribe what to do and are identified with "must," "ought," "should," "would," or their equivalent without qualification (Bustrillos, 1963, p. 46).

No decision is independent of time. Each decision has historical perspective. One must, therefore, be able to perceive events and phenomenon in a *time relationship* because it is this perception which gives meaning and continuity to events. This time base may be the past, present, or the future (Bustrillos, 1963, p. 8). Statements about the traditional, the habitual, or a reference to what had gone before (such as: "I used to —," "I experienced") indicate the past. When statements are based on what is on-going but not habitual, on what one feels or thinks at the moment, the time reference is present. Predictive statements of fulfillment of a future state of affairs (such as: "in the future," "tomorrow," "I expect it to happen," "if they —") denote the future (Bustrillos, 1963, p. 47).

### Decision-Making Rule

Decision-making rule consists of the method by which alternative courses of action are evaluated. Decision-making rules are used to differentiate alternatives and to arrive at a choice.

Bustrillos identified three decision-making rules: preference ranking, objective elimination, and immediate closure. (Bustrillos, 1963, pp. 8-10). *Preference ranking* involves the ordinal ranking of perceived alternatives. Alternatives are evaluated and placed in order from best to worst, according to a subjectively defined criterion. Harries describes this rule as

> essentially a *lexicographic* ordering approach, in which a decision-maker ranks or evaluates alternatives with respect to values placed on an alternative's most important attribute. If more than one alternative exhibits the same value for the most important attribute, the tie is broken by looking at the second most important attribute, and so on until there are either no more ties or no more attributes. All perceived alternatives are thus ranked according to the decision-maker's preference along several dimensions (Harries, 1972, p. 9).

In *objective elimination* the decision is quickly recognized because it is based on the limits imposed by the immediate environment. No one best alternative is consistently chosen; the best depends on the conditions obtaining (Bustrillos, 1963, pp. 9-10). Alternatives are qualified with phrases such as: "under these conditions _ is best;" "but if _, then _." The decision maker maintains an objective rather than subjective stance.

The objective elimination rule can be likened to the *satisficing rule* developed by Simon (1957) in that it suggests that the decision maker will choose the first alternative that exceeds a set of minimal criteria. A decision will be made that is "good enough," and the decision maker is aware that the decision will have a measure of both sacrifice and satisfaction. Using the satisficing rule, a decision maker "uses fewer dimensions and perhaps operates at a lower level of complexity in processing information than with a preference or lexicographic ordering model. In the latter model, all perceived alternatives are ranked according to preference along several dimensions, which requires integration and differentiation of information" (Harries, 1972, pp. 10-11).

In *immediate closure* only one action is focused upon. The single alternative is immediately grasped without explicit ranking or elimination. The process is quick; rationalization comes after making the decision. The rule may indicate a low level of information processing.

The *satislex rule* developed by Russ (1971) combines satisficing and lexicographic ordering. The decision maker will determine the degree of satisfaction and sacrifice of each alternative and then place these in order of preference.

Some decision makers can process more complex information than others. Harries ranked decision rules according to complexity of information processing required. Ranked in order from simplest to most complex they were; (1) immediate closure, (2) preference ranking or satisficing, (3) lexicographic ordering, and (4) satislex.

Competence in processing information and making decisions becomes increasingly important as increased amounts of information become a part of daily living. Understanding how information is processed may help decision makers in their decision making.

## HABITUAL AND NEW RESPONSES

At some point all decisions involve conscious behavior. As a result of past learning, much decision behavior becomes routine and can be carried out almost automatically; it becomes habitual. A suitable response is simply drawn from memory and very little conscious decision making effort is involved. For example, a family may have worked out a breakfast pattern with which each member is satisfied. Choices must be made as to what kind of fruit or juice will be served and how the eggs will be cooked but these decisions become habitual in time.

Some decisions seem impulsive or intuitive. A selection or resolution is reached immediately with seemingly little conscious identification or weighing of alternatives. The selection may be based on "accumulation of experience, pleasant or unpleasant; a keen observation of what others have gone through" (Bustrillos, 1963, p. 96). The decision maker tends to consider more aspects of the problem than can be verbalized. The situation is viewed in an overall fashion. The decision is readily rationalized and the decision maker tends to verbalize general satisfaction. When the situation has new elements, the need for conscious, deliberate decision arises. For example, conflict may arise if a teen-age daughter decides not to eat any breakfast. Her mother's value of health may be in opposition to the daughter's desire for independence and a slim figure. Breakfast becomes an area for conscious decision.

Habitual and new responses have been viewed as nonprogrammed and programmed decisions. "Decisions are nonprogrammed to the extent that they are novel, unstructured, and consequential" (Simon, 1960, p. 6). Nonprogrammed decisions range from rather minor ones to those of a critical nature. They can be simple or complex. They are challenging because they represent unstructured, new situations. Sometimes they call for adaptation or modifying one's pattern of behavior. Sometimes innovation is necessary to find the correct approach or reach an unfulfilled goal. Consequences often are far-reaching. The decision making is characterized by an organic unity of interrelated parts forming a whole that is larger than the sum of its parts.

Decisions that require new kinds of responses vary in complexity. For example, the McIntyre family has never had a garden. Since this is a new situation for them and it involves some potential sources of conflict, they must consider such questions as: Who will be responsible for looking after the garden? What will be sacrificed in order to find time for gardening? What new skills will be required of family members?

Some of the most important decisions are made only once or just a few times in a lifetime. Their consequences may be irrevocable, as when the family is confronted with the possibility of having a child's leg amputated. Medical technology has made it possible to make awesome decisions, such as when someone shall be born, and when life shall end. Other kinds of decisions are quite easily revoked. A family can join a book club that requires the purchase of three books during the first year and then the membership can be dropped. To revoke some decisions is more complicated but possible (e.g., a will that establishes a revocable trust can be changed but is likely to require legal assistance).

Some decisions are very complex, involve a high degree of risk and uncertainty, and may have serious consequences. For example, a homemaker may decide to look for a part-time job when she is in her mid-thirties. Viewed as a simple choice between being a part-time employee or a full-time homemaker, she can justify seeking employment because it would boost her sense of self-fulfillment. When she considers her choice as part of the environmental setting, the decision becomes more complex. Additional decisions will need to be made such as: How will the family use the additional income? Which job will she take? Who will care for the children, prepare the meals, shop, and do the cleaning? Complex decisions often are surrounded by uncertainty. Multiple factors are interacting with each other.

Creative thinking and projections of possible outcomes in regard to future consequences need consideration. Seeking part-time employment could require changes in the homemaker's orientation. She might have to meet a firm time schedule on her job, develop proficiency or skills beyond her present level, find easier or more convenient methods of completing her homemaking duties, and reduce the frequency with which she does certain tasks. Changes in the physical environment may be desirable; such as purchasing new labor-saving equipment, substituting commercial services instead of doing things herself, using convenience foods, or simplifying living by reducing time spent in housecleaning, or changing her style of entertaining.

Decisions are programmed to the extent that they are repetitive and routine, to the extent that a definite procedure has been worked out for handling them so they don't have to be treated *de novo* each time they occur (Simon, 1960, pp. 5-6).

Repetitive decisions depend on having in mind information about a number of feasible alternatives and making the decision from among these general alternatives. Many everyday family activities are programmed: how to prepare food, shopping for groceries, ways for paying bills. Programmed decisions are based on stored information and can become routine or habitual. Nonprogrammed decisions require new information. They occur when the situation has new information that upsets the equilibrium between the decision maker and the environment. Conflict is present.

Conflict situations abound in everyday family living. They occur when family members note that the values held by individuals within a family conflict with those held by other individuals both inside and outside the family; when what is being accomplished is not consistent with what the family as a whole or individual family members believe ought to be accomplished; when there is disparity between goals and resources. Such conflicts are brought about by changes in the environment (e.g., introduction of new technology, occupational or income changes, or in developmental changes in family members). Decision situations may be concerned "primarily with appraisal and reorganization or adjusted control of activities involved in the use of resources. Or the decision situation may center upon one or more forms of interaction among family members (i.e., conflict between actual and desired effectiveness of communication networks, role patterns or ways of performing certain types of activities can trigger the need for decision)" (Paolucci, 1966b, p. 339).

## TYPES OF DECISIONS

Decisions may be classified according to formal properties or substantive characteristics. Formal properties refer to theoretical or abstract characteristics that are independent of content, for example, degree of rationality. Substantive characteristics are related to the nature of the problem; that is, whether it is social, economic, or technical. Knowing the decision type can be helpful in determining the degree of rationality needed for making a particular decision.

### Formal Properties

The basis for making conscious choice is rationality—the ability to order information in an objective and logical manner. Researchers (Baker, et al., 1973), building on the work of Halliday (1964), have developed a model for viewing and scoring degrees of rationality used in arriving at decisions in hypothetical family decision situations. The model identifies five dimensions of rationality: (1) diagnostic orientation, (2) number of alternatives, (3) comparing or ranking alternatives, (4) inquiry for and use of information, and (5) total response.

In a study of families of Mexican descent (responses of husband-wife pairs were analyzed), Baker (1974) found that decision makers were more rational in identifying alternatives than they were in ranking them; in determining the overall situation than they were in diagnosing the source or cause of a decision problem. Decision rationality varied with decision situation (see Table 2).

It has been found that the degree of rationality present is situation specific; that is the decision process varies with the particular family decision (Glass, 1961; Bustrillos, 1963; Halliday, 1964; Baker et al., 1973; and Baker, 1974). One could say that all decisions need not be charted by the same map.

### Substantive Characteristics

The type of decision warranted can be related to the nature of the decision situation: social, economic, or technical. Diesing (1962, pp. 244-247) indicates that these decision situations differ in their approach to reason: (1) reason as creativity, which he relates to *social decisions*, and (2) reason as calculating, literally adding and subtract-

**Table 2**
Continuum of Decision Rationality
(Variations in Decision Dimensions by Family Decision Situations; Mean Scores, $N = 34$)

| Dimensions | Situations | | | | | | | Mean Scores, All Situations |
|---|---|---|---|---|---|---|---|---|
| | Trip to Mexico | Family Size | Community Involvement | School | Economics and Work | Illness and Surgery | | |
| Total response | 1.82 | 2.00 | 2.15 | 1.59 | 2.08 | 1.44 | | 1.85 |
| Diagnostic orientation | 1.06 | 1.50 | 0.59 | 0.76 | 0.79 | 0.24 | | 0.82 |
| Number of alternatives | 2.32 | 1.53 | 2.20 | 1.82 | 1.88 | 1.73 | | 1.91 |
| Ranking alternatives | 1.79 | 1.65 | 1.67 | 1.97 | 1.65 | 1.32 | | 1.68 |
| Use of information | 2.15 | 1.76 | 1.79 | 1.94 | 1.26 | 1.65 | | 1.76 |
| Total score— all dimensions | 9.14 | 8.44 | 8.40 | 8.08 | 7.66 | 6.38 | | 8.02 |

*Note:* The highest score assigned to a dimension was 3; with five decision categories, 15 would be the highest total score for an individual respondent, and a mean score of 15 the highest score for a family (husband–wife pairs) on any one decision situation.
*Source:* Georgianne Baker, "Decision Profiles of Mexican Descent Families." Paper presented at Annual Meeting of National Council of Family Relations, St. Louis, Missouri, October 1974, p. 5 (mimeographed). Reprinted with permission of author).

101

ing and comparing costs and benefits, which he relates to *economic* and *technical decisions.*

*Social decision making* occurs when the family encounters conflict in values, goals, or roles of family members. The conflict can be internal for a family member; social decisions then involve the roles an individual will assume, the specific content of these roles, and the manner in which these roles will be integrated into a consistent self (Price, 1969). More generally the value, goal, and role conflicts occur between and among family members or the family unit and other social groups such as the school or the family service agencies.

Social decisions are integrative in nature; their purpose is to bring the family group to some level of unity. Here the decision does not consist of selecting one particular alternative because it best maximizes a given goal, but rather the decision is one of creating a goal, alternative, or course of action out of an indefinite number of possibilities present in the decision situation. The decision is a result of mediation rather than selection. In mediation a melding rather than selection or rejection occurs. In a social conflict situation a predetermined goal for the social group is not present; goals emerge as a part of the decision process. In this kind of situation, typical in a family decision where the consequences impringe on more than one person, the choice becomes one of changing the values, goals, or roles involved and adjusting other psychocultural factors to arrive at some level of resolution. The process is one of order and direction of change. New alternatives are derived from the separate alternatives perceived by each member of the decision-making group. Hence, the alternative that emerges will be limited by the perceptions of the particular group members.

The following conflict situations illustrate that individual family members tend to push for a solution that meets only their own needs. The key to social decision making, however, is for the people to work together creatively to find an answer that can satisfy all of them. The process involves developing as many potential solutions as possible. Melding takes place and a new alternative arises that can best meet everyone's needs.

Example 1: Mark and Jack were sharing an apartment while attending college. Mark liked to study evenings but Jack considered evenings to be "party time." They discussed several possible solutions but each led them into further arguments:

1. Mark should spend several evenings a week studying at the university library.
2. Jack should party at his friends' homes.
3. Mark should get by without studying in the evening if he used his free hours between classes effectively.
4. Jack should get better grades by studying more and cutting down on his parties.

Can you imagine which person might have suggested each of these possibilities? Can you see why they were not really solutions but simply led to further disagreements? Notice how judgmental these suggestions are. The implications are that Mark studies too much and shouldn't expect to do it at home and that Jack should spend more time studying and less time partying. The "shoulds" are a denial of their individual needs and freedom.

Finally a new alternative was created that recognized the differences in Mark's and Jack's interests while acknowledging that they had equal rights to the use of their apartment evenings. The key elements of this solution were:

1. Mark would study at a friend's home or at the university library on Monday and Wednesday evenings so Jack could do whatever he wished at home.
2. Jack would either be away from the apartment or be quiet at home on Tuesday and Thursday evenings so Mark could study there.
3. Friday, Saturday, and Sunday evenings Mark and Jack could party together or negotiate from week to week so their individual desires could be satisfied at home.

Example 2: Elaine and Ruth were sharing an apartment during their first year of work after graduation from college. Elaine wanted the apartment to be neat and clean at all times. When they agreed to live together, they decided to split the cleaning equally. Soon Elaine found herself doing most of the cleaning and even picking up Ruth's clutter. In talking about the problem, Elaine insisted that Ruth live up to their original agreement and do her half of the cleaning. Ruth said she hated to clean. She suggested that they divide the cost of cleaning help every week or two. Elaine said she could not afford the additional expense; it was difficult enough to make her limited resources stretch to cover her current monthly expenses. Ruth admitted that Elaine ended up doing most of the work. After considerable discussion, a new alternative evolved that was acceptable to both. Ruth proposed that, in some way, she could compensate by doing other tasks that she found more enjoyable than cleaning. Elaine thought that sounded fair. They decided that Ruth would do the weekly shopping and a little more than half of the cooking. Since Elaine didn't have a car, she was happy to be relieved of the shopping.

Example 3: Sherri and Barney were both employed. Barney expected Sherri to pay the bills from her paycheck. Sherri resented the way Barney spent money on his friends and business associates, ignored the bills, borrowed money, and got deeper into debt all the time. Sherri's constant worrying about money bothered Barney. Endless discussions seemed to get nowhere. In an effort to find a solution they both could live with, they sat down and wrote all the alternatives they could think of:

1. Sherri learns not to worry so much about money.
2. Barney stops treating his friends and going into debt.
3. Sherri and Barney discuss each expenditure of $10 or more before it is made.
4. Sherri quits her job to force them to live from Barney's earnings.

None of these suggestions seemed workable. Neither Sherri nor Barney could change their personalities over night, as alternatives 1 and 2 would require. They tried alternative 3 and it caused more disagreements. Number 4 really wouldn't solve the basic problem.

After much brainstorming, they came up with a fifth alternative that sounded good to both of them:

Each month they would set aside a certain amount of money Barney could use to treat his friends and business associates. Likewise, Sherri could count on a specific allowance to spend any way she wished. They would work together in planning a budget based on their total income so as to cover current bills and make payments toward reducing their debts. Neither would incur further debt without discussing it in advance with the other.

In social decision making the conflicts. . . are resolved by a process in which *desires are changed rather than satisfied* and alternative actions are chosen according to how they contribute to bringing about the change and bringing the unit to some level of integration so that individuals can function as units (become an integrated family). . . . The approaches used can be those of (1) reconciling factors that once were in conflict by arriving at a consensus; (2) coming to a compromise wherein different individuals tolerate parts of all the conflicting factors, or (3) compartmentalizing the conflicting factors and operating in an inconsistent manner; that is, as if the conflicts did not in fact exist. In any case, successful social decision-making leads to increased integration of the group (Paolucci, 1966a, p. 4).

*Economic decisions* are decisions that involve assessment and allocation. They require ordering, evaluating, and selecting means and goals when goals are either complementary or competitive. Goals are evaluated by *comparing* the returns possible for each alternative in a given situation. The goal selected is that which promises to yield greatest return from available resources. A single goal may be chosen, or several goals may be rank ordered. Achieving one goal implies sacrificing another. The goals must be comparable on some scale. In economic decision making the decision maker is aware of and thus can compare several goals. It requires that available resources be known and in some degree measurable so they can be objectively allocated. A number of approaches for arriving at the decision are possible. They can range from an approach based on the degree of knowledge one has in relation to the degree of risk one is willing to take to the use of game theory strategies. Procedures can be highly subjective or mathematically objective. Although any number of approaches for arriving at the decision are possible, decisions always involve selecting one alternative and rejecting all others.

*Technical decisions* are ways of implementing social and economic decisions. They focus on the procedures to carry out the decisions that are made. They concern ways of carrying out family activities and accomplishing daily tasks. Once the "best" way has been determined, the carrying out can become routine and may no longer require conscious, deliberate decision.

These decisions seem to be relatively inconsequential but together they make up the family's pattern of life. Failure in implementing decisions reduces the family's decision making power. Difficulty in carrying out decisions may be reflected in apathy when future decisions arise.

Once the differences in family values have been resolved (social decision) and the goals have been selected in accordance with the limited resources (economic decision), technical decisions raise such questions as: *What* needs to be done to carry out this goal? *Where* should it be done? *When* should it be done? *How* can it be done best? *Who* should do it? These questions relate to systematizing the "deciding and the doing" to carry out family living harmoniously and expeditiously.


## INTERRELATEDNESS OF FAMILY DECISIONS

Decision making is a dynamic process in which the decision makers and the decision situations change. Yet, decision making is characterized by a web of connections or organic unity in which the parts form a whole that is larger than the sum of its parts. Decisions, especially those that are complex, are interrelated and interdependent. Two patterns have been conceptualized that show decision linkage: central satellite and chain (Paolucci, 1963: Plonk, 1968; Bean, 1968; Myers, 1967).

Scheme 1: Central—Satellite

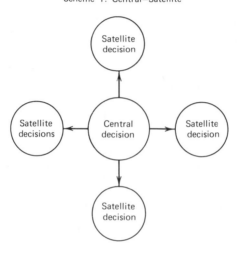

Scheme 2: Chain

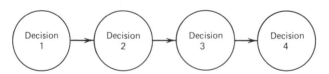

Figure 9. Decision Linkage

## Central-Satellite Pattern

Figure 9 illustrates the central-satellite pattern characterized by a significant central choice with several minor choices dependent on and related to it. The family encounters many situations in which a strategic choice is the basis for making other choices. For example, one's choice of occupation can be the central factor in choosing where the family lives, how much money is available, with whom the family members will associate, and what kinds of family activities can be shared.

The decision a couple makes to have a child is a central decision. Satellite choices related to the kind of environment in which that child will grow affect the "success" of the central choice; the central choice also affects many satellite decisions the new parents will make about their own life style.

Since the central choice is the pivot for several satellite choices, it must be made with great care. Rational decision making requires considerable time and effort to seek feasible alternatives, gather information on their effectiveness, weigh each alternative, and select what appears to be the best one in light of the known consequences.

Likewise, satellite choices can determine the nature and quality of the central choice. Not only is each choice an end in itself but it is instrumental in fulfilling an important goal. Small decisions about daily household routines can add up to a successful or unsuccessful central choice. These decisions may appear to be trivial when viewed separately but together they result in a smoothly functioning household. For some families, focusing on the smaller choices is a desirable way to bring about central choices of quality.

A central choice is crucial to the satellite choices it generates. Plonk (1968) studied decision linkage among persons who were moving to retirement housing. She described the kinds of supplemental satellite decisions that were needed to execute a strategic (or central) decision:

A *tactical decision* is an instrumental decision that begins or continues action to complete the core idea. It sets limits and boundaries for other decisions (e.g., selecting a particular apartment in a retirement housing project; selecting a color scheme).

A *policy decision* is a plan for handling certain decision-demanding situations that might arise (e.g., where to have guest meals, house overnight guests, entertain large groups).

A *control decision* regulates, changes, facilitates, simplifies, or adjusts a decision in any of the satellite classes and enables the action started in other decisions to continue (e.g., selectively eliminating surplus furnishings or memorabilia collected over a lifetime).

A *program decision* establishes a new routine for the regularly recurring activities in the new situation (e.g., selecting times, planning how to get personal laundry done).

Plonk (1968) summarized the content linkage of decisions that were instrumental in a retirement housing decision in this way: transporting (setting the moving date, moving possessions, traveling to new residence); choosing the unit (size and location of the unit in the building); establishing the unit (selecting and placing furniture, choosing colors for apartment and furnishings, lodging while purchasing or waiting for furniture); living patterns (policies about guests, medical service, group activity, routines for daily living and self maintenance); reducing possessions (dispostion of furniture, family treasures, real estate, car); establishing self (involvement in retirement housing community, activities, business contacts).

Reallocation of resources may follow a central choice. For example, Harry just graduated from high school. During his senior year he spent half a day in a work experience program specializing in engine tune-up. He has been saving some of his money to buy a sports car. When he learned recently that he is to be the father of a baby who will be born in about six months, he suggested that he and Olga get married. She has accepted. They have discussed some of the satellite decisions such as their living arrangements, her completion of high school, and his job. Harry is just beginning to realize that his decision to get married requires many changes in the use of his resources. The money he had hoped to save for a sports car will be reallocated to pay the baby's expenses. The room and board he was paying his parents will go toward renting an apartment. He will have to find a full-time job to pay the rest of the rent and the food costs. Even the apportionment of his time will require some adjustments— he won't be able to spend every weekend with his friends overhauling old cars. Maybe he should consider going to the regional occupational center evenings to broaden his skills in auto mechanics. As energetic as he is, he begins to wonder how he can keep up with a family, a full-time job, night school, and still find time to see his friends.

Chain Pattern

As shown in Figure 9, a chain pattern is characterized by a straight line, sequential dependence of one decision upon another. Each decision is directly dependent on the preceding choice. The chain can stop and recommence at any point. For example, consider the dependence of each choice on the previous choice in constructing a garment; selection of a pattern determines the kinds of fabrics that are possible, the fabric determines the construction techniques, construction techniques determine the necessary sewing skill and the time and effort to be expended.

Sometimes decisions are time-ordered and they constitute a chain pattern. For example, when Jane was in high school she enjoyed her chemistry course, in college she became enthused by her nutrition courses and decided to major in that field. Her master's degree prepared her to work in public health nutrition and her first full-time position was with a county public health department. Notice how dependent each step in Jane's sequence was upon the preceding step. Note too that although each choice she made opened new options, they also drastically reduced the occupational alternatives open to her—she accumulated experience that she would not want to waste. She enlarged her social commitments, yet defined more narrowly what her first position might be.

Complex decisions may involve a combination of related and interdependent decisions tied to a strategic decision. The retirement housing example mentioned several kinds of satellite decisions, one of which concerned the plans for transportation. Within the transportation class, you can see a chain pattern: the moving date had to be set before the possessions were moved to the new apartment.

When a situation is complex, it may be helpful to take one step at a time. Gradually the chain builds into a pattern. Sometimes minor parts of a decision can be identified and dealt with in some order of priority.

Understanding the web of decision situations can be helpful in recognizing consequences, new opportunities, and future constraints opened by a central choice, as well as in relating these to both family members and their environment.

## FAMILY DECISION MAKERS

Decision making in families does not fall to one family member; rather the task is shared at some level by each family member. At times the decision is made by a member acting for the family; at other times family members make the decision conjointly or several members may collaborate in making choices. Research abounds concerning *who* in the family makes decisions (Rainwater, 1959; Heer, 1963; Blood and Wolfe, 1960; Olson, 1969; Komarovsky, 1967; Safilios-Rothschild, 1969 and 1970; Centers and Raven, 1971 and Sawer, 1973). Generally, who makes the decision depends on the family's expectation of role; that is, who in the family *should* decide; who in the family has "power" by virtue of age, sex, competence, earning ability, or propinquity (whoever is in the situation when the decision must be made).

Who makes the family decision may differ in different stages of the decision process. For example, the father may decide on how much money is to be spent on food, but the mother makes the actual decision when she shops for groceries; or parents decide how late adolescents may stay out at night, but each adolescent decides as the decision is implemented.

Participation in family decision making seems to be critical to whether the decision will be accepted and carried out (Turner, 1970, pp. 97-116). The family offers many opportunities for each member to share in the decision process. By so doing, each individual can air opinions, make suggestions, and vote on a decision before it becomes effective. Through conjoint discussion among family members, each can come to agreement upon the choice and become committed to its implementation.

Group participation, however, is not necessary or appropriate in handling every decision that arises within the family. Rather trivial problems can be handled as they arise. At the opposite extreme, it is conceivable that certain vital decisions can only be made by the person or persons really qualified to make them. If this is the case, these individuals should share their plans with the others as soon as they can and explain as much as the others need to know for them to accept the decision. The effectiveness of a decision depends on two factors—quality and acceptability. If either factor is lacking it would seem that a decision would be less than effective. Preferably, both will be high but a decision can be effective if either one is high.

## SUMMARY

Decision making in the family is not a simple process. Rather, it involves the complex interplay of decision makers, specific decision situations, and various rules for choice making. At one point, ends are determined through the process of mediation of values and goals; at another point specific goals are linked to resources to form complimentary or competitive alternatives; lastly, particular means are used to achieve a selected goal. Family decisions do not occur in isolation; rather one decision is inextricably tied to another in a continuous means-end chain.

## SELECTED REFERENCES

Baker, Georgianne. "Decision Profiles of Mexican-Descent Families." Paper given at annual meeting of National Conference on Family Relations, St. Louis, Missouri, 1974.

Baker, G., L. Recinose, and V. Mejia-Pivaral. "Family Planning Variables in Four Guatemalan Villages." Proceedings of Annual Latin American Conference of Arizona Latin American Studies, Center for Latin American Studies, Arizona State University (mimeo.), 1973.

Bean, Nancy M. "Decision Class, Linkage, and Sequence in One Central-Satellite Decision Complex: Students' Summer Occupational Choice." Unpublished Master's thesis, Michigan State University, 1968.

Blood, Robert O., and D. M. Wolfe. *Husbands and Wives: Dynamics of Married Living.* Glencoe, Ill.: The Free Press, 1960.

Bustrillos, Nena. "Decision-making Styles of Selected Mexican Homemakers." Unpublished Ph.D. dissertation, Michigan State University, 1963.

Centers, Richard, and Bertram H. Raven. "Conjugal Power Structure: A Re-Examination." *American Sociological Review.* 36 (April 1971): 264-278.

Diesing, Paul. *Reason in Society: Five Types of Decisions and Their Social Conditions.* Urbana, Ill.: University of Illinois Press, 1962.

Glass, David C. "An Empirical Application of Formal Decision Theory to Parent Decision-making." *Journal of Psychological Studies.* 12, 5 (1961): 188-207.

Halliday, Jean. "Relationships Among Certain Characteristics of a Decision Event: Decision Procedure, Decision Context, and Decision-Maker." Unpublished Ph.D. dissertation, Michigan State University, 1964.

Harries, Nancy G. "The Effect of a Programmed Course of Instruction on the Development of Information-Processing Competence and Decision-making Styles." Unpublished Ph.D. dissertation, Michigan State University, 1972.

Heer, D. M. "The Measurement and Bases of Family Power: An Overview." *Marriage and Family Living.* 25 (1963): 133-139.

Hoyt, Elizabeth E. *Choice and the Destiny of Nations*. New York: Philosophical Library, 1969.

Komarovsky, Mirra. *Blue-Collar Marriage*. New York: Randon House, 1967.

Kuhn, Alfred. *The Logic of Social Systems*. San Francisco: Jossey-Bass, 1974.

Meyers, Anna Mae. "Class and Interrelatedness of Decisions Ensuing from the Decisions of Wives to Seek Employment." Unpublished M.A. thesis, Virginia Polytechnic Institute, 1967.

Olson, David H. "The Measurement of Power Using Self-Report and Behavioral Methods." *Journal of Marriage and the Family*, 31 (1969): 545-550.

Paolucci, Beatrice. "Family Decision-making." Paper presented at seminar sponsored by the Department of Household Economics and Management, Cornell University, Ithaca, New York, May 8, 1966a.

Paolucci, Beatrice. "Contributions of a Framework of Home Management to the Teaching of Family Relationships." *Journal of Marriage and the Family*. 28, 3 (August 1966b): 339.

Paolucci, Beatrice. "Managerial Decision Patterns." *Penney's Fashions and Fabrics*. (Fall/Winter 1963).

Plonk, Martha A. "Exploring Interrelationships in a Central-Satellite Decision Complex." *Journal of Home Economics*. 60 (December 1968): 789-792.

Price, Dorothy. "Social Decision-Making." In *The Family: Focus on Management*. Proceedings of a National Conference, Washington, D.C., American Home Economics Association, 1969, p. 14.

Rainwater, Lee. *Workingman's Wife*. Oceana Publications, Dobbs Ferry, N.Y., 1959.

Russ, F. A. "Consumer Evaluation of Alternative Product Models." Unpublished Ph.D. dissertation, Carnegie-Mellon University, 1971.

Safilios-Rothschild, Constantina. "Family Sociology or Wives' Family Sociology? A Cross-Cultural Examination of Decision-Making." *Journal of Marriage and the Family*. 31 (May 1969): 290-301.

Safilios-Rothschild, Constantina. "The Study of Family Power Structure: A Review of 1960-69." *Journal of Marriage and the Family*. 32 (November 1970): 539-552.

Sawer, Barbara J. "Predictors of the Farm Wife's Involvement in General Management and Adoption Decisions." *Rural Sociology*. 38, 4 (Winter 1973): 412-426.

Simon, Herbert A. *Models of Man*. New York: John Wiley & Sons, 1957.

Simon, Herbert A. *The New Science of Management Decision*. New York: Harper and Row, 1960, pp. 5-6.

Turner, Ralph H. *Family Interaction*. New York: John Wiley & Sons, Inc., 1970.

# Chapter 7
# Reducing Uncertainty in Decision Making

The quality of deliberate, conscious decisions the family makes reflects the capacity of the family organization to process information effectively. Information processing, the perception, selection, exchange, and attachment of meaning to informational stimuli in the environment, is the essence of family decision making. The degree to which the family is able to make effective decisions depends on its ability to perceive, code, and transmit information. Information reduces uncertainty and facilitates the prediction and control of family events. Effective information processing assures smooth family functioning; inability to process information results in disorder and dissatisfaction in family functioning. A task of the family organization is to develop guides or rules for handling information.

Information is the basic ingredient of decision making. It is the image of the environment the family member holds. Through the stimuli of the human senses, the matter-energy of environments is structured and patterned into recognizable concepts that "make sense" or have meaning to the person. When those concepts are structured and have the same meaning for more than one person, when the information is a "shared experience," communication exists among the persons who share the meaning. Commonality of informational data and similar perceptions of those data provide the basis for family decisions. The degree to which this communication exists either assures that acceptable decisions will be made and carried out or determines the degree of uncertainty—lack of understanding and meaning—that will surround a given decision and its outcome. Uncertainty can be viewed as a mismatch between information that family members or groups have retained in their memory from past experiences compared with what they perceive in present situations. *Reducing uncertainty* is a process of matching information from the environment with memory. This matching occurs as decision makers perceive their environments, compare these perceptions with memory of past experiences, adjust the perception by either adding to or adjusting memory or by reinterpreting the environment, and, on the basis of this matching, act.

The amount of information transmitted depends on the extent of knowledge held by the person who is to receive the information. If Bob tells his preschooler that the fruit she is having for breakfast is a banana, and Sally already knew that, Sally has gained no information. On the other hand, if Sally has never had papaya and Bob tells her that this is papaya, information is transmitted. Sally was totally uncertain as to what kind of fruit she was eating; Bob's communication reduced that uncertainty.

An ability to process information, to reduce uncertainty, is intrinsic and essential to human survival.


## INTRINSIC MOTIVATION FOR INFORMATION PROCESSING

A major goal of the family is to teach its members to decide: to cope with routine and new problems, to seek information and deal with uncertainty, and to process information in new and meaningful ways. Family members who develop these skills have a basis for adapting to a changing environment and making creative decisions.

When these skills are poorly developed, family members are likely to look to external authorities for solutions to their problems and for standards by which to judge behavior. They allow others to determine what is "right" or "wrong" and "good" or "bad." They blame others or outside forces when something goes wrong and credit them when things go right. They lose their intrinsic wonder, curiosity, and creativity. Boredom increases. Decisions are made either by relying on past experience of self or others. The tendency to avoid uncertainty and ambiguity is accompanied by a view of the world as fixed and out of the control of the family (Carza, 1974).

Family members, however, need not depend on persons external to the family for information upon which to base choices. Families often find highly complex and incongruent situations more challenging than situations that are familiar and almost completely congruent. They are motivated by an urge to master the situation. Their curiosity is stimulated by a moderate level of incongruity or novelty.

Intrinsically motivated persons have their own "built in" system of rewards and punishments. Their motivation is based on ability to sense discrepancies or mismatches in the various perspectives they consider. These discrepancies—incongruities in the environment—act as stimulators, according to Schroder (1973, p. 45). Individuals can motivate themselves by forming new concepts, and by creating uncertainty and conflicting judgments. The conflict or discrepancy that is generated stimulates an exploration of the conflicting possibilities.

The more complex situations enable family members to see the same information in different ways. When outcomes can be surprising, interest might be sustained longer than if an expected outcome is probable. Skill in processing information helps the decision maker see and appreciate differences and generate new insights from the same information. The family can help its members develop intrinsic motivation if it provides opportunities for choice. The family can provide support and security for its members as they search, inquire and try out different ways of perceiving, deciding, and behaving.


## INFORMATION PROCESSING

Each person carries internally a cognitive map of the environment containing stored information from past experiences that helps one adapt to that environment. For example, a woman purchased a beautiful, all-purpose coat but she noticed, after wearing it on a very rainy day, that one side had shrunk. The next time she purchased a coat to be worn in rainy weather, she recalled the facts about unsuitable fabrics and placed greater value on the efficiency of the raincoat than on its attractiveness.

### Information Overload

When the environment is relatively stable, a person has a chance to adjust to changes gradually. In the twentieth century, however, the environment changes rapidly, irregularly, and unpredictably and provides humans with a "glut" of information. According to Toffler (1970) and Miller (1965), a person has limited ability to receive, process, and remember information. When the system is overloaded, a serious breakdown of performance can result.

The number of options available is related to the length of time it takes to reach a decision and carry it out. Even without understanding its potential impact, we are accelerating the generalized rate of change in society. We are forcing people to adapt to a new life pace, to confront novel situations and master them in ever shorter intervals. We are forcing them to choose among fast-multiplying options. We are, in other words, forcing them to process information at a far more rapid pace than was necessary in slowly evolving societies. There can be little doubt that we are subjecting at least some of them to cognitive overstimulation.*

A family needs to find ways to reduce options in some arenas of family living. Because Tom is color blind, he asked his wife to prepare a color-coordinated chart of his shirts and ties. Tom can choose from among 12 ties that are on Mary's coordinated list. In order to select the right tie, Tom needs some information. If, with the shirt he has chosen, Mary's list eliminates the plaid tie, this information reduces to 11 the number of ties from which he can choose. If the chart indicates that the first four ties on the left of the tie rack can be worn with the shirt, his alternatives are reduced from 12 to 4. If the chart shows that the third tie is coordinated best with a particular suit and shirt, he has all the information he needs. How helpful information is depends on the percentage of alternatives it eliminates.

A family's ability to process information is related to the ways in which the family adapts to the environment. "The essence of the organism's interaction with the world is the identification and acquisition of potentially useful stimuli, the translation and transforma-

*From *Future Shock* by Alvin Toffler. Copyright 1970 by Random House.

tion received into meaningful patterns, and the use of these patterns in choosing an optimal response" (Schroder and Suedfeld, 1971, p. 3). Defense mechanisms, such as avoidance and denial, and perceptual rigidity are means of preventing information from flowing into the family. Since families are continually bombarded with information, they have to learn to be selective when determining what information they will process. Much information is quickly forgotten; that which is remembered becomes schematized, relatively logical, and well conceptualized. Miller (1965, p. 367) has suggested some ways for partially handling information overload. These include: (1) deliberately screening out or ignoring some information, (2) putting information in priority by filtering out that which is essential for the here and now from that which is considered nonessential, (3) making selections on the basis of previously determined value hierarchies or goals, (4) abstracting or attending to information in broad sweeps rather than giving attention to detail, and (5) chunking or putting like information together to form generalizations.

### Information Constraints

Another way of reducing information overload and hence uncertainty is to place constraints on the number of alternatives to be considered or the detail of information about each alternative. The concept of constraint is used to refer to the arbitrary limits placed on information about alternatives. A family might wish to purchase a new automobile that would average 30 or more miles per gallon of gas. From the list of information about all current models of automobiles, this family would confine itself to seeking information only about that set of cars that meet the mileage criteria.

Constraint occurs whenever the set is deliberately made smaller than it might be. When the decision set does not offer the full range of alternatives, there are fewer degrees of freedom for choice. The importance of degrees of freedom can be understood by noting that the four legs of a chair have 24 degrees of freedom before they are assembled; that is, before constraint is placed upon them. If three legs are placed in position, then the position of the fourth has no degrees of freedom; where it goes is predictable. So it is with alternatives, the fewer the possibilities, the fewer the degrees of freedom. Uncertainty is greater when the range of possibilities is greater. Deliberately introducing constraints reduces uncertainty.

### Cognitive Complexity

Family members' perceptions of the world are related to their information-processing ability. Those with well-developed information-processing skills have a larger number of perceptual categories through which to receive information about the world. They have the ability to *generate more information* relative to their needs and to use rules or concepts to combine and organize units of information. It is important that family decision makers acquire the ability to generate information and to organize it so that it can become a guide for making decisions. Families could help each member develop skills in information generation and concept formation and utilization.

Schroder (1973, pp. 28–39) has categorized persons as either concrete or complex information processors and has contrasted their characteristics. Persons lacking complex information-processing skills have few degrees of freedom in dealing with the environment. They use simple and fixed rules in designing courses of action. They are not able to generate a diversity of information in a variety of ways for decision making purposes. Individuals with low levels of information-processing ability are often intolerant of ambiguity, dogmatic, rigid, and closed-minded. They are concrete processors. They are dependent on external authority and externally defined rules; they are often inflexible in their attitudes and categorical in their thinking.

Persons with complex information-processing skills, on the other hand, can modulate transactions with the environment. They are, in many ways, mirror images of the persons lacking skills in information processing: they have many degrees of freedom in dealing with the world. They are active manipulators of their environment. They generate their own rules for coping with problems and are attuned, adaptive, and flexible in the face of change and uncertainty. Such individuals have many ways to organize sensory inputs, to mediate them, and to respond to them. They are capable of entertaining and processing alternative explanations of an event and seek diversity and discrepant material in their information processing. They are complex processors. With such skills, one can begin to appreciate how the complex information-processing organization would be better suited to successful survival in a rapidly changing, complex world; better prepared to cope with different groups they encounter; and better able to generate decisions more appropriate for a diverse and changing society.

Adaptation to a changing environment is enhanced when the family feels free to explore the world and seek new information. High-level decision making can take place when the family organization is capable of organizing units of information, viewing them in several different ways and utilizing them in deciding.

## INFORMATION ACCESSIBILITY, COST, AND CREDIBILITY

### Information Accessibility

How accessible is the information on which to base family decisions? On one hand the family is bombarded with information from many sources: mass media, schools, advertising. On the other hand, appropriate information may be inaccessible because of the decision maker's inability to decode the information. Inability to read or understand what is said because of learning or language barriers makes information inaccessible.

In addition, information may be inaccessible because it is limited or not available at the time it is needed. For example, Sharon wanted to invest in something that would provide a tax shelter for her family. One possibility was to get into a limited partnership that was planning to develop a new golf course. The prospectus gave predictions as to the number of players and income the golf course might expect. Nevertheless, the information was limited since no factual data could be obtained until the golf course actually opened. Sharon also considered two tax-sheltered annuities, one of which was "no load" and paid 7% interest (meaning the family would receive 7% on the full amount invested). The other plan charged an initial fee of 6% (off the "top" of each investment) and paid 8% interest on the remainder of the investment. Both plans stated a minimum guaranteed level of interest, well below the amount being paid at the time. Sharon wanted information that was not available such as the rate of interest she could expect a year or five years from now. Also, she had to work out for herself how many years it would take for the two annuity plans to return the same benefits and which plan would return greater profit, in the long run, for the length of time her family might wish to maintain a tax-sheltered annuity. Unpredictable factors, such as the family's health and occupational status in future years, made the family very much aware of the inaccessibility of information at times when decisions are being made.

### Cost of Information

Time needed to acquire the information and the fee paid for expert information (e.g., medical advice) can be costly. Families often make decisions on the basis of cost of information. In fact, searching for information over a long period of time may result in a choice made by default. For example, one might search for so long for all information needed to decide upon a new position that another person could be hired while the decision maker was acquiring information! Family decision makers need to develop skill in determining when searching for new or more information may enhance or hinder the decision potentials.

### Information Credibility

Information in complex environments becomes increasingly difficult to assimilate because messages from many sources become mixed. Complex situations may contain various and discrepant facts and opinions. When conflicting messages come from government offices or from research institutes, a "credibility gap" forms. Family decision makers find it both frustrating and costly to deal with the information. An ability to deal with ambiguity becomes essential.

Some of the major ways in which families react when information is conceptually in conflict have been identified by Berlyne (1960, pp. 286-288). These include: (1) doubt—when one can both believe and disbelieve the same statement; (2) perplexity—when there is no way of knowing with certainty which of several mutually exclusive beliefs is true; (3) contradiction—when overt expressions of others violates the laws of thought or logic of an individual; (4) incongruity—when information one perceives is not congruent with what one believes ought to exist; (5) confusion—when ambiguous information patterning causes one to act in an unpredictable manner and (6) irrelevance—when one is unable to connect one's own thinking to that of other people; in the family, when one member sees information as relevant to a situation while others do not.

Information credibility can be cognitively enhanced through

denial, bolstering, differentiating, or transcendence (Berlyne, 1960, pp. 284-285). Through *denial* one can change the evaluation of some elements of information, (e.g., daughter would like to be slim and yet eat rich desserts; since she cannot satisfy both likes, she professes that she never liked rich desserts anyway). A smoker, worried about lung cancer, decides smoking is a bad habit and costs too much money by *bolstering* information. He links one bit of information with another that is associated with strong attitudes and thus has enough information to outweigh the opposing belief. By differentiating within sets of conflicting information one is able to both positively and negatively value the information. For example, belief in the truth of the Bible and in the theory of evolution is reconciled by differentiating literal and figurative truth and attributing only figurative truth to the Bible. Conflicting information can be *transcended* by combining information into a larger unit that is viewed with favor or disfavor (e.g., a partiality for both science and religion, perceived in opposite directions, may give rise to the feeling that a well-rounded life requires cultivation of both).

### Risk and Uncertainty

*Risk* refers to a decision situation in which probabilities of outcomes can be attached to the possible alternatives. These may be objective probabilities or they may be simply an individual's appraisal of the amount of satisfaction he or she would obtain by taking a certain action. The degree of risk is related to the availability of accurate information. *Uncertainty*, on the other hand, indicates the decision maker has limited knowledge or information concerning the probabilities of certain outcomes or the satisfaction he or she will obtain from a particular action. With uncertain information, risk is greater.

Families who purchase insurance probably have a negative expectation of ever needing to use it. If all families did need insurance the insurance companies would go bankrupt. Yet, rational people generally agree with the importance of having insurance. By taking insurance, individuals are paying so as *not* to take risks. They are willing to accept as fair insurance a given money cost rather than risk the more serious loss against which they are insuring. At times a sound decision may be one of taking the greater risk of loss and not spending money on insurance premiums because it may result in a greater gain. However, the decision makers need to be aware of the chances they are taking. A lottery also has negative expected value but the individual pays in order to take a risk. The expected utility of a winning ticket is greater than the certain loss of the cost of the ticket.

Family decision makers can deal with uncertainty in several ways. Several devices are listed here. Limit the series of possibilities and work out a strategy in advance for each possibility (e.g., a home-maker who is unfamiliar with prices of several foods on her market list can work out a range of acceptable prices for meat, vegetables, fruits). If a definite range of possibilities exists, apply a strategy that will result in minimum loss if things work out badly and a maximum gain if they work well (e.g., Linda was planning a celebration for her mother's 90th birthday. Her aunt suggested having an open house and inviting many friends; the aunt and some cousins would be available to help. Linda decided not to attempt something so large. As it turned out, illness and a snow storm kept Linda's aunt and cousins home; had Linda given an open house she would have had to manage alone. Her decision to have a turkey dinner for the relatives provided a satisfying celebration with less fatigue and cost than the open house would have involved).

If uncertainty is completely indefinite but promises to be only temporary, deal with it by increasing the liquidity of one's assets. As uncertainty is reduced, change strategy rapidly (e.g., a family expecting to move to an uncertain destination within three years can maintain high liquidity—rent instead of buy a house, cultivate only superficial friendships or learn how to handle separations and endings, maintain broad interests). If uncertainty is to begin at a definite future time, give preference to ends that are achievable before the uncertainty period begins. As hedges against uncertainty, avoid decisive acts when knowledge is inadequate, postpone irretriev-able decisions by not acting at all or by fitting acts into a variety of developments, and watch for signals that will clarify the situation and permit more decisive actions (Diesing, 1962, pp. 55, 97).


## STRATEGIES FOR CHOICE

Many heuristic methods have been developed for selecting one alter-native over another; for handling information so that it becomes meaningful and useful for making a decision. Ways of handling information may be considered strategies for selecting alternatives. These strategies suggest guides for comparing information about alternative possibilities and choosing the one that will yield the greatest satisfaction or least dissatisfaction or regret. David W. Miller and Martin K. Starr have identified a number of strategies in *The Structure of Human Decision* (1967).

### Pro and Con

One of the simplest strategies is that of identifying and analyzing possible alternatives on the basis of their advantages and disadvantages or costs and benefits. To do this write the decision situation at the top of a piece of paper, draw a line down the middle, making two columns. Head one column Pro (benefits) and the other Con (costs). When possible, allow at least three or four days to think of every pertinent idea or the different motives appropriate for one column or the other. Carry the paper around, jotting down the ideas as they come. Weigh all the ideas for their relative importance. Write the conclusion at the bottom of the page. For important decisions, file the Pro and Con sheets so that later, if the correctness of a decision is questioned, you can establish the reasoning behind what was done. Or more important, commit the information to memory to be used in other similar decision situations.

Viewing the Pro and Con arguments together enables the family to evaluate a situation better, thereby reducing some of the chance or whim that might otherwise be operating. L. Nicholas Roosevelt (in *A Front Row Seat*) illustrated using this approach when he and his wife were considering whether to move from New York to Big Sur. They listed what they considered the desirable and undesirable consequences of the move, thus:

| *Desirable/PRO* | *Undesirable/CON* |
|---|---|
| Better health | Loss of interesting contacts |
| Release from overwork | Separation from relatives and friends |
| Chance to write | Reduced income probable |
| End of stultifying routine | Time-consuming chores |
| More beautiful surroundings | Housework without help |

*From *A Front Row Seat*, by Nicholas Roosevelt. Copyright 1953 by the University of Oklahoma Press.

They chose to move and found even greater satisfaction than they expected.

### Maximim

For some decisions, the family decision maker may want to be guided by comparing the amount of pain or pleasure a decision might generate. The maximim strategy is based on the theory that the decision maker will try to maximize the desirable or pleasurable aspects of the choice. The less desirable aspects will be minimized. Basically, this is an application of the psychological principle that the goal of human action is to seek pleasure and avoid pain.

One problem inherent in this approach is that all the courses of action open are not always known. Even if they were known, one would not be able to predict the outcomes of all actions. One could calculate probabilities but still be confused about which consequences would be satisfying. Because human beings are not perfectly consistent or sensitive, they do not always choose the alternative that is "best" from an objective standpoint.

Frequently one alternative is not best on all dimensions. Perhaps a family finds two houses that are equal in cost. One is in a better location and the other is more solidly constructed. The family members would balance one attribute against the other. Their decision would be based on the relative weight they assign to each of these characteristics.

When time is considered very important, a family tends to choose between alternative actions in such a way that satisfaction will be obtained as quickly as possible. This may not result in maximum long-range satisfaction, however. As an example, a college student, Ron, spends almost every evening at his girl friend's home and finds he doesn't have time to keep up with his college work. Ron proposes marriage to Lisa with the idea that their immediate satisfaction would be greater in marriage and he might be able to find more time to study if he didn't have to travel to and from her house each evening. This may be a short-range solution to the problem, but if Lisa's pregnancy following marriage means that Ron has to quit school entirely to earn enough money to support Lisa and the baby, the decision to marry may not provide long-range satisfaction.

Another dimension of this principle is to select the course of action that is expected to yield the greatest return for the least commitment of resources, whether these are financial, material, human, or temporal. One version of this is to choose the alternative that would require the least expenditure of resources to achieve the goal. Another variation is to decide on a specific level of expenditure and select the option that one expects would lead to the greatest goal achievement.

Under the *maximin principle*, the most attractive option may be chosen in terms of the one most likely to lead to the defined goal, yield the greatest return for the resources expended, or offer the greatest satisfaction. It may produce the least pain, loss, or inconvenience.

Sometimes the family is willing to accept less than the best in order to realize the most probable outcome. For instance, a firm offers Fred higher salary than he now earns to work on a government contract that will last for two years. His present employer is unwilling to grant him a leave of absence or give him a raise. His wife is expecting their third child. Should he choose the lower pay with greater job security and fringe benefits or should he accept the higher paying, temporary job and risk having to find another job two years from now?

### Minimax

A similar principle states that, among the possible alternatives, one choice has the worst consequences or the smallest payoff. The aim is to minimize one's maximum losses. Actually the minimax and maximin principles lead to the same choice when the most satisfactory alternative is the option that *maximizes the minimum payoff.* For example, Tim has an opportunity to purchase a tax-sheltered annuity through the school system by which he is employed. He could select a fixed annuity that would guarantee to return the money he invests plus a fixed rate of interest. Or, he could invest in a variable annuity that might increase much more rapidly or might decrease sharply in value. Using the minimax principle, he would select the fixed plan that gives a higher guaranteed level, thereby making his minimum payoff as high as possible. His choice might be equivalent to what he would make under the maximin principle of selecting the alternative that would be most desirable or have the *maximum expected value*, in his view. On the other hand, if Tim's financial condition is such that he can afford to take some risk and he evaluates the probability of certain outcomes, he might decide that the variable plan offers sufficiently more promise of greater return to make it worth the risk of greater loss.

The *minimax regret principle* calls attention to the fact that a person may wish later that a different option had been chosen. The amount of regret is related to the difference between the payoff that is received for the choice made and the payoff that might have been obtained. If the option with maximum payoff was chosen, regret would be zero. The aim is to minimize the maximum regret.

Trying to feel out the position that will yield the most satisfaction with the least discomfort is a balancing act. The theory is to decide on the maximum acceptable loss—the boundary loss—and the minimum acceptable gain that would make the action worthwhile—the boundary gain. Two conditions have to be met: (1) The lowest relevant outcome must be more attractive than the boundary loss or the family will be afraid to take a risk that cannot be afforded; and (2) the highest relevant outcome must be greater than the boundary gain or a person will lack the incentive to take a risk.

Family decision makers develop guides for selecting alternatives that provide the most satisfaction and cause them the least dissatisfaction. At the point of making the decision, they act as if they have complete information; as if they are certain. In general, family decision makers try to select that alternative that provides them with the largest payoff at the least cost.

Uncertainty and risk are inherent in making family choices, for information is never complete or totally accurate for the specific situation. Understanding how information is related to decision making should be helpful to families as they develop their own guides for sorting information for making everyday family choices.

## SUMMARY

Being able to predict or shape the direction of interactions between family members and environments is dependent upon the information families have for making decisions. As environments become more complex, more information is generated. It becomes increasingly difficult for families to understand this information and to sort it so that it has meaning and utility for them. The risks based on uncertainty of information can be reduced by learning to process information. If family decision makers are to use information effectively, they must become adept at complex information processing or decide to restrict information inputs through simplifying environments.

## SELECTED REFERENCES

Berlyne, D. E. *Conflict, Arousal, and Curiosity.* New York: McGraw-Hill, 1960.

Carza, Raymond T., and Russell E. Ames, Jr. "A Comparison of Chicanos and Anglos on Locus of Control." Paper presented at 46th annual convention of the Midwestern Psychological Association, Chicago, Illinois, May 1974.

Diesing, Paul. *Reason in Society.* Urbana: University of Illinois Press, 1962.

Miller, D. W., and M. K. Starr. *The Structure of Human Decisions.* Englewood Cliffs, N. J. Prentice-Hall, 1967.

Miller, James G. "Living Systems: Structure and Process." *Behavioral Science.* 10 (October, 1965): 337–399.

Roosevelt, L. Nicholas. *A Front Row Seat.* Norman: University of Oklahoma Press, 1953.

Schroder, Harold, Marvin Karlins, Jacqueline Phares. *Education for Freedom.* New York: John Wiley & Sons, 1973.

Schroder, Harold M., and Peter Suedfeld. *Personality Theory and Information Processing.* New York: The Ronald Press, 1971.

Toffler, Alvin. *Future Shock.* New York: Random House, 1970.

# Chapter 8
# Managing Resources to Achieve Goals

Results of interactions between families and their near environments can be a matter of chance, or they can be managed. This chapter takes the position that families can learn to manage resources in order to achieve goals. This will encourage the optimum development of family members and maintain a viable environment. Crucial to management is an understanding of the role of values, goals, and standards as basic information, either in the form of stored experiences or as new responses to environmental stimuli, to the shaping of particular actions. Management in the family is viewed as continuous processes of family-environment transactions that are determined by the family organization.

The family organization concerns itself with the management or informed control of life. The family organizes resources to mediate values and attain specific family goals. It gives attention to the conscious recognition of diverse and common goals of family members and the deliberate allocation, creation, and use of resources. This managerial activity includes making plans based on value clarification, goal setting, standard setting, and resource allocation, as well as implementing plans through facilitating, checking, and adjusting actions generated to carry out specific activities (see Figure 10).

128

## DECISION MAKING

Decision making is a basic activity of the family organization. It is concerned with integrating values, goals, standards, and resources in such a fashion that action results.

### Value Clarifying

Values are the base for goals. "It is clear that values as such are not goals or objectives . . . . They are not the things sought, but they are what gives the sought-after things importance. People use them as norms and criteria that point the way to goals and objectives." (Fitcher, 1957, p. 301). Specifications of goals and the specific criteria or standard necessary for determining whether or not the goal has been attained is value-based. Therefore values must be brought to a level of awareness, clarified, and internalized at a level of commitment that allows them to serve as a base of worthwhile goals.

To have a value is to be able to give reasons for motivating goal-oriented behavior in terms of benefits and costs, bringing to bear explicitly a conception of what is in a man's interests and what goes against his interest: to operate within reason—giving contexts with reference to a "vision of the good life." Valuation is an instrumentality of a "life world" (*Lebenswelt*) of rational agents endowed with pro-feelings and con-feelings and thus possessing the capacity for goal-directed behavior in a social (i.e., reciprocally communicative) setting (Rescher, 1969, p. 10).

What the family values enters indirectly into what the family says it wants to pursue (family members' verbalizations and rationalizations of certain covert actions). Values, manifested in overt action, are reflected in the goals pursued. The reasons for taking the action are verbalized and thus the action is justified. In a sense this is a looking backward, an evaluation, of the past action. These rationalizations form a part of the stored information, or memory, that is retrieved when making new decisions and taking action in the future. This is a reflective process by which the "past" shapes the "present" and, at the level of planning, the "future."

There are many strategies for clarifying values. They range from

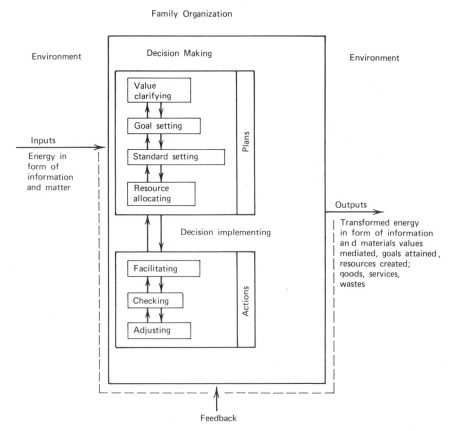

Figure 10. Adaptive Processes of the Family Organization

so-called "forced choice" techniques (i.e., forcing one to take a position on a controversial issue) to analysis of how families spend resources of time, energy, or money (i.e., budget analysis coupled with the *reasons for* the expenditures). If goals are to be consciously *selected* and *pursued*, it is essential for the family to know what it values. (Formation and classification of values were discussed in Chapter 4.)

### Value-Goal Relationships

Goals form a chain that leads to the realization of values. As various goals interlock, some of them become ends toward which lesser goals are directed. Deliberate decision making is a mechanism for choosing between alternate goals and selecting the order in which they are to be pursued.

Without a value system at their core, goals could be aimless and confused. Values provide a steadying influence that gives direction to goals. Goals are highly specific. Progress in attaining them can be observed; their achievement can be recognized.

As an example of how values shape goals, think of a young couple with two preschool children. The husband has high *economic* values. He is concerned about the practical problem of what would happen to his family in the event of his death. He could translate his value into a number of specific goals, one of which might be to purchase a life insurance policy to provide for his survivors. Family decisions often involve the interaction of several values and many possible goals. Consider the complexity of some of the questions this family would need to work out: Should the father be concerned merely with providing for the minimum needs of his wife and children for a limited period, say five years? Should he make provision for the children to be able to attend college? Is a bare existence level of living all that he should provide or should he allow for the development of any creative abilities the children might have? If he attempts to provide beyond the minimum level, can his family afford the heavy cost of insurance now? What kind of insurance policy would be the best buy for the type of coverage his family needs? When he settles on a particular policy, should he make payments annually, semi-annually, quarterly, or weekly? These questions reveal how economic, aesthetic, and social values contrast with what appears to be a simple goal.

### Goal Setting

Goal setting is a necessary activity of the open, complex family organization. The attention given to internal and external interchanges between family members and between the family unit and other systems affects the ability of the family organization to set goals that help adapt members to their environment.

The kinds of goals families set are directly related to the resources available to the family. Weick (1971, pp. 25-30) has suggested that goal setting develops over time in four somewhat developmental stages: (1) diverse ends leading to common means where achievement of the diverse goals of individual family members depends on access to common resources; (2) common means leading to common ends where common family resources are used to pursue composite or group goals; (3) common ends leading to diverse means where common goals utilize the resources of particular family members for achievement; and (4) diverse means leading to diverse ends where individual family members pursue individual goals through use of their individual resources. The common means leading to common ends stage represents a high level of integration, while the diverse means leading to diverse ends stage represents a low level of integration.

Goal setting is a dynamic activity. Through the continuous balancing of means and ends the family establishes a complex of goals "which is made up of many goals in various stages—some nearing completion, some being formed, and still others which may endure for a lifetime . . . . This goal-complex serves as a reference point for the family's managerial action and . . . as a guide in determining the direction and the selection of means for managerial action" (Gross et al., 1973, p. 282).

Goal setting is always cast in a future orientation; the degree of "futurism" varies among goals. Some goals can be accomplished in relatively short time; others may take years to achieve. The ability to set long-term or short-term goals may be related to how the family views its control over circumstances. Rotter (1971) contends that family members differ in their tendency to attribute satisfactions and failures to themselves rather than to external causes: highly external persons feel they are at the mercy of the environment, that they are being manipulated by outside forces and their goals are externally determined. If they set goals; they tend to be short-range ones. Internally motivated persons, on the other hand, feel they are in control; they are "free" to set goals, think in terms of the future and long-range goals. They can both adapt the environment and adapt to it.

Goals vary in their concreteness or abstractness. For example, purchasing an automobile is tangible, concrete, but the goal of developing harmonious interpersonal relationships is more abstract.

The setting of goals requires adequate processing of information from both the external environment and from family members. Family situations must be created that will allow each person to contribute, according to current capabilities, to the establishment of goals that are satisfying and acceptable to all. Open and free communication can be encouraged so that family members can become sensitive to the desires of others and willing to express their particular wants and needs.

Through its goal-setting activity, the family organization formulates a goal complex, which Edwards (1970, p. 653) describes as providing "overall direction for system behavior, and in terms of which subsequent family behavior becomes understandable."

Setting acceptable and achievable family goals will require consideration of the following factors: diversity and commonality of means and ends, complexity, duration, and a sense of control.

### Standard Setting

Standards are criteria, guidelines, or specifications of goals; they have their origin in values. Specifically, they are measures of "quality and/or quantity which reflects reconciliation of resources with demands" (Maloch and Deacon, 1966, p. 33). They are critical to management activity for they provide the base for determining the outcomes of the family organization system. Standards reflect the decisions made by family members as they mediate values and set goals: they are "an agreed-upon measure of quantity, quality, performance, or achievement" (Paolucci et al., 1973, p. 41).

Standards fall into two general categories: conventional and scientific. *Conventional* or traditional standards have their base in the larger environment. They have been accepted by the family over a period of time and are relatively fixed. Conventional ways of behaving may have been adopted because they are convenient, economical, or because of social pressure. Tradition is deep-rooted, with much of it stemming from within the family and immediate culture groups. Standards that are embedded in the environment are not changed easily. At the same time, they may not be the most appropriate or efficient standards for a particular situation.

In the process of setting standards, conflict may arise between those family members who have accepted conventional standards and others who would choose to ignore them. For example, the standards that a parent finds acceptable may differ from those accepted by adolescents. For Bob, a college sophomore, the "good life" is found in a casual life style: faded clothing, sexual freedom, emphasis on the nonmaterial and experimental. In contrast, Bob's parents define the "good life" in terms of conventional clothing, "sex within the marriage bond," emphasis on the comfortable, convenient, material, and "tried" rather than experimental. Standards for acceptable behavior are determined in the family through interchanges of information and question raising. For example: Should these parents force Bob to adopt their standard because it is a conventional way of determining acceptability? Should they allow him to evolve his own standard with the idea that each individual has the right to make decisions and bear the consequences of his choice? It is through this communication process that standards are determined in the family. If consensus is reached, a new standard will have emerged that is acceptable to both Bob and his parents. Otherwise, standards with varying degrees of acceptability will emerge. The family's ability to establish standard's in part depends on how acceptable proposed standards are to its members.

Feedback from family members and the cultural environment result in family standards that are particular to each situation and flexible in nature. Flexible standards are built on the idea that no single standard is equally suited to all individuals, families, or situations. Rather, multiple standards exist. What is best in one family differs from what is reasonable for another. What is appropriate at one time for a given family may not be appropriate at other times. For example, most families hold certain minimum standards of cleanliness. Yet, each family must decide what this minimum is for its home by considering such factors as the number, ages, and health of the family members, their interests and activities, the size of the house and its conditions, their cleaning equipment and its efficiency, the climate, and season of the year. When the family members agree on reasonable standards and decide how the work will be distributed to attain the standards, they are likely to cooperate in fulfilling them. The evolved standard indicates what the family members consider to be essential.

Families are influenced by scientific discoveries and the impact of scientific information. Research in the physical and behavioral sciences has been directed toward setting *scientific standards* for physical well-being as well as for the products and services used by families. Government standards have been established to protect and inform consumers. Scientific standards have been developed in areas such as nutrient and caloric needs of humans, acceptable levels of bacterial count, thread count and tensile strength of fabrics, minimum floor space, light and construction of housing, flammability of children's clothing, safety of toys, pollution emission of automobiles.

Descriptive data can give a picture of typical practices among families of a certain income level and living in a particular geographical region. These data provide information ranging from expenditures to sexual behavior. These practices can be viewed as standards. When viewed in terms of what they actually represent, such data can be helpful. They should not be misconstrued, however, as reflecting standards or practices that families ought to follow. In this sense these standards are more conventional than scientific.

If standards are to be used as yardsticks for judging whether goals have been achieved, they must be stated in *measurable* terms. Scientific information can be used to objectively quantify many standards. Examples of quantitative measures are: accepted levels of expenditures, such as amounts of money to be expended for specific family items or energy to be comsumed (kilowatts, B.T.U.s, gallons of gasoline) in operating the household; nutrients and calories needed to meet nutritional adequacy; amount of time spent to perform given family tasks.

Standards "measured" in qualitative terms are often comparatively expressed and tend to be subjective. Such standards are defined on continuums of high or low, more or less. Examples of qualitative standards include "quality of life" described in terms of degrees of freedom, happiness, love, health; educability defined as skills needed to succeed in school. Qualitative standards describe what the family considers to be essential; family members will exert effort to secure them and feel dissatisfied and uncomfortable about if they are not attained. Feelings of discomfort if something is not achieved and continued effort to procure are the "real test of whether or not something is a standard . . . this inner conviction of what is important . . ." (Gross, et al., 1973, p. 133).

Vickers (1970, p. 126) notes that standards continually grow and change with communication—the key for achieving shared standards:

> For we should not spend so much time in committees, board meetings, legislative sessions and so on if we did not believe that talking to each other made a difference, not only by communicating facts, but also by changing each other's standards—including our own—of what is important and how it should be evaluated.

This is also true in families. The *shared* standard is achieved through communication and mutual understanding.

Managerial activity within the family would be simpler, but not necessarily more effective, if all family members shared the same goals and standards. It is, however, the transacting of ideas, the very process of mediating that takes place among family members that leads to flexibility and diversity of family goals. This diversity gives the family more options, allows each family member to be independent in initiating action yet interdependent on other family members for responding so that the action can be carried out. This interlocking of family member to family member is critical to giving stability —a sense of cohesion—to the family group.

It is most difficult, in an intimate group such as the family, to refrain from imposing one's own standards and values on another. It could be beneficial, therefore, to appraise the origin of a family's standards, how satisfying they are to the group and to each individual, how much they cost in terms of human and nonhuman resources, and what effects achieving them may have on others.

Because standards are "specifications of values" (Gross et al., 1973, p. 128) they have their origins in the environments of family members. They are, however, formed specifically for the family situation through intrafamily transactions among family members and interactions that interlock the near environment. Standards accepted by the family are influenced by the cultural milieu and by the scientific environment. They are set by the family to meet their specific criteria and depend on information flows and feedback between the family organization and the larger environment.

### Resource Allocation

Stated simply, family resources are what the family has or can create to get what it wants. They are means to ends. Matter-energy is the basic family resource; however, in order for matter-energy to be useful to the family it must be perceived as information and converted into a form that will allow specific goals to be achieved (i.e., food, gasoline, electricity, information, clothing, houses, material goods). A family resource, then, is matter-energy that has been converted into a specific form for use in attaining a family goal.

Family resources can be classified as human and nonhuman. *Human resources* include all of the values, attitudes, abilities, human energy, knowledge, and skills the family members possess. Values and attitudes are learned; they are *motivators* (i.e., they activate a person to seek certain ends). Abilities can be innate or learned. Human energy is the force or power to work or to act. Knowledge refers not just to an accumulation of facts but to the ability to see functional relationships between them. Skills refer to proficiency in activities that involve the use of mind and body; they range from skill in playing a musical instrument or repairing a piece of equipment to caring for children or resolving interpersonal conflicts. Nonhuman resources include money, facilities, and material objects available to the family.

If resources are to be utilized they must be known and their usefulness recognized. The personal attribute of ability to recognize and effectively use resources is known as *resourcefulness* (Baker, 1970, pp. 42–47). It involves:

1) the use of technical knowledge to deal with economic resources; thus, the home manager has the "know-how" to work with things such as material goods and services, i.e., food, clothing, furnishings, equipment. 2) the use of social knowledge to deal with the non-economic resources; thus, the home manager has the sensitivity and "know-how" to work with individuals within and outside the household, such as understanding needs, abilities and skills (Wetters, 1970, p. 7).

Resource Attributes

To be used, resources need to be *allocated* and *exchanged. Allocation* is a distribution of resources among alternative ends. It is an impersonal procedure dealing with means and ends. *Exchange* is a transfer of resources between persons or groups. It is usually based on bargaining, which is the social procedure involving two socially related economic units. such as between and among persons within and outside the family; between and among families and other social and economic systems (Diesing, 1962, p. 43; Scanzoni, 1972).

Resources are interchangeable; that is, one resource can be substituted for another to achieve a given end, or the same end could be achieved by using different resources. Resources are also interrelated and/or interdependent: success in performing a task is related to ability, knowledge, and the object needed for performance; i.e. a particular material object (computer) is dependent upon information (knowledge) if it is to be useful.

Resources can be exchanged through two- or one-way transfers.

A *two-way* transfer refers to those exchanges in which there is a contractual reciprocal arrangement; for example, exchanges of specific amount of money for a particular item or of given number of hours of work for certain sums of money or services. These transfers usually utilize market mechanisms. In two-way transfers there is immediate reciprocity; a resource is given and a resource is received simultaneously. *One-way* transfers usually occur outside the marketplace. Boulding (1973, p. 1) has referred to these one-way transfers as the grants economy. Grants are used to connote the idea that one-way transfers do not involve immediate or contractual reciprocity. They can occur between family members, or from one family to another, from business to a family or individual, from government to individual, from governments to governments. The basic idea is that the exchange does not have immediate reciprocity nor is it contractual in nature. A grant, however, may in fact involve reciprocity over time. Boulding (1973, p. 26) identifies this as serial reciprocity. For example, parents may provide a child with money for education and the child may then provide parents with housing at some future time or may provide education for another family member. Such arrangements are separate parts of the same transaction but the reciprocity is implicit rather than explicit; it is not contractual and, in fact, may not be expected. One-way transfers can be made for either benevolent or malevolent reasons; out of love or fear. Hence, their effects can be either positive or negative. Positive effects of one-way transfers are feelings of goodwill, trust, and affection; negative effects can create the opposite or malevolent effects. One-way transfers within the family can help build trust and serve as an important integrating function for the family and between families and the rest of society. One-way transfers in the family, make a significant economic contribution, as well as important noneconomic contributions. Baerwaldt and Morgan (1973) have estimated the 1970 magnitude of interfamily transfers (gifts from one family to another where a relationship was not involved) as $8.4 billion dollars; intrafamily transfers (transfers among family members) as $313.2 billion dollars. Bivens (1975) has identified four ways families make one-way transfers or grants to their members: (1) by providing physical sustenance as well as intangible items such as education, leisure experiences, and emotional support; (2) by bestowing facilitating know-how, that is, the ability to know what to do in a given situation such as seeking a career or carrying out a new role; (3) by assisting family members to venture into ever-widening social situations that involve the ability to cope constructively with risk and uncertainty; and (4) by assisting with value and attitude formation.

Foa (1971) has attempted to bridge the dichotomy between resources, to view the attributes of transferability, interdependence, and interrelatedness by interpreting interpersonal behavior as an exchange, characterized by profit and loss. This idea of exchange produces difficulties, however, because resources such as information and love can be given to others without reducing the amount possessed by the giver. Therefore, Foa developed a theory to allow different resources to follow distinct rules of exchange. Interpersonal (human) resources and economic resources were classified by Foa (1971, p. 346) as (1) love, viewed as an expression of affectionate regard, worth, or comfort; (2) status as evaluative judgments that convey high or low prestige, regard, or esteem; (3) information offered as advice, opinions, instruction, or enlightenment, but exclusive of those behaviors that could be classed as love or status; (4) money as coins, currency, or tokens that have some standard unit of exchange value; (5) goods such as tangible products, objects, or materials; and (6) services defined as activities performed on the body or belongings of a person usually constituting labor of one person for another.

These resources can be classified on a concrete to symbolic or a particularistic to universal scale (see Figure 11). *Concrete* behavior is described as giving an object or performing an activity that affects that body or belongings of another individual. *Symbolic* behavior refers to language or nonverbal behavior such as body posture, gesture, or facial expression (Foa, 1971, p. 346). For example, services and goods are considered concrete because they involve the exchange of a tangible activity or product; status and information, conveyed by verbal and nonverbal behaviors, are more symbolic. Love and money are exchanged in both concrete and symbolic forms, and thus occupy intermediate positions on the scale. *Particularistic* behaviors are actions of a person who is relatively significant; a parent, spouse, or friend are highly specific. *Universal* behavior occurs at the opposite end of the scale; the person who renders the service is relatively insignificant (e.g., the identity of the bank teller is not important to the depositor). Love is at the extreme particularistic position because it matters a great deal from whom we receive love and its reinforcing effectiveness is closely tied to the person who gives it. Money is at the universal end since it can retain the same value regardless of the

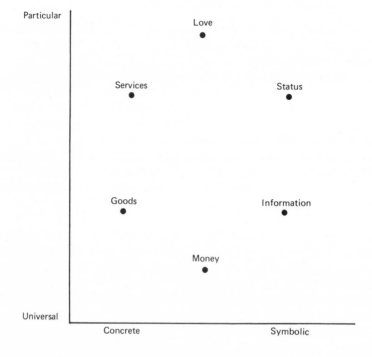

**Figure 11.** Exchangeability of Noneconomic and Economic Resources (Adapted from "Interpersonal and Economic Resources," by U. G. Foa, *Science*, Vol. 171, pp. 345-351, Fig. 29, January 1971. Copyright 1971 by the American Association for the Advancement of Science.)

relation between, or characteristics of, the giver and receiver. In the middle range, services and status are more similar to love while information and goals are closer to money (Foa, 1971, p. 346).

Resources that are near one another in the scale are more substitutable, or more appropriately exchanged, those that are far apart are less so. Similar rules of exchange may be applicable to two close resources while different rules would exist for the exchange of more distant resources. The more particular the resource, the greater the probability that it will be exchanged with the same resource; nonparticularistic resources tend to be exchanged with different ones. (Foa and Foa, 1974, p. 164). Six exchange properties have been identified and related to the position of the resources. The first two properties refer to exchange outcomes and the others are concerned with environmental conditions that enhance or hinder particular exchanges (Foa, 1971, pp. 348-349).

1. *Relationship between self and other.* The relationship between giving the resource to another and giving it to self is positive for love but diminishes and becomes negative as one moves from love toward money. This is related to the notion that the ability to love others requires self-acceptance and self-love. Money, on the other hand, is opposite since one person's gain is another's loss. Consequently, an exchange of money can result in gain or loss while an exchange of love cannot.

2. *Relationship between giving and taking.* Love usually involves a certain degree of ambivalence; giving love can occur in the presence of some hostility or the taking away of love. Giving and taking away money is, however, not likely to occur at the same time.

3. *Relationship between interpersonal situation and exchange.* Money can be exchanged through a third person. It does not require an interpersonal relationship in order to be transferred or kept for future uses. Love, however, cannot be separated from the persons involved, kept for a long time without actual exchange, or transferred by an intermediary.

4. *Time for processing input.* Giving and receiving love requires time. It cannot be hurried. Money, on the other hand, can be exchanged very rapidly.

5. *Delay of reward.* Building love takes a relatively long time. Rewards come usually after repeated encounters; trust (the expectation that the exchange will be completed) is a necessary condition. Exchanging money with another resource can be done in a single episode.

6. *Optimum group size.* There may be an optimum group size for exchange of particular resources. Love functions best in small groups and is particularistic while money can function in large groups.

The relationship between resources and their concrete and symbolic and particular and universal attributes may

originate in the sequence of cognitive development . . . during socialization . . . . Love develops early, in the small and relatively permanent family group, before the "self-other" and "giving-taking" differentiations have become firmly established. Money, on the other hand, acquires its meaning much later, after one has learned that "self" is not "other" and "giving" is not "taking," and from the beginning it is used mostly for exchanges outside the family. Thus resources are best exchanged in conditions that resemble those under which they had been learned in the past (Foa, 1971, p. 349).

This resource exchange framework helps explain decisions made by families that may be misjudged by the outsider. Only if the needs of particular families are understood can the decision related to resource exchanges be understood. The framework can be helpful also in making decisions about how to best use the human resources of the family. For example, when should the resource used be particularistic and when should it be universal? What differences in human development and family relationships occur when the particularistic human resource of the mother's or father's time and energy is used rather than the universal resource of the caretaker's time and energy at a child-care center?

One of the important transformations that occurs within the family is that of creating or developing human resources. In fact, the building of human skills, attitudes, and values, which occurs through family interaction, is viewed as a basic and indispensible function of the family. This human resource development is the family's investment in the future and its major contribution to the larger social system: the development of human capital.

The quality of the human capital produced depends on the quality of the environment in which the family organization interacts and the quality of decisions made within the family organization system. Principles of guidance long used in child development reflect the potential for decision making in the family that leads to the development of human resources with the capacity for making productive contributions in the larger environment. Family members foster values through the ways they chose to approve or disapprove one another's actions. They build abilities by helping and encouraging one another. Feelings of self-respect are encouraged and fostered by accepting individual differences, and security is developed by a mutual sharing of affection (see Figure 12).

The optimum development of the human resource seems to depend on the consistent reinforcement of an individual's behavior in a secure and dependable environment. The interactions that occur in the particularistic environment between particular persons offer one of the best possibilities for human resource development. The Waring

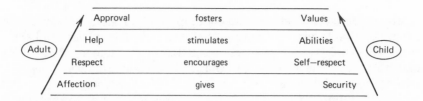

| Adult | | | | Child |
|---|---|---|---|---|
| | Approval | fosters | Values | |
| | Help | stimulates | Abilities | |
| | Respect | encourages | Self—respect | |
| | Affection | gives | Security | |

Figure 12. Guidance Principle: Relationship Between Guidance and Child's Need (Reprinted from "Principles of Child Guidance" by Ethel Waring, a publication of the N.Y.S. College of Human Ecology, a Statutory College of the State University, Cornell University, Ithaca, N. Y.)

schema expanded to include all family members as they interact in the family setting could assure the development of those particularistic human resources of love, status, and service now in short supply in our more universalistic society.

### Resource Limitations

Resources are scarce or limited, at least at particular points in time and space. Some resources, such as fossil fuels, are believed to be finite. Most resources are expendable; that is, if they are used for one purpose they are not available for use in another situation. The human resources, however, can be conceptualized in one sense as expandable. Families can "create" human resources (new persons) and can build their potential, which, with use, increases rather than diminishes. Knowledge, love, and empathy, for example, increase with use.

### Resource Measures

If resources are to be allocated effectively they must in some way be measureable. Their availability and utility need to be determined readily. Limits as well as uses need to be judged in relation to specific goals. Both quantitative and qualitative dimensions need to be assessed. Some measurements (such as amount of time, kind and amount of energy or money) are objective measures that can be used to quantify a cluster of interrelated resources. For example, household work takes time, it also encourages the use of skill, knowledge, ability, human energy, and materials to perform a task. Other measures are more subjective in nature and encompass qualitative measures; for example, the level or standard that was reached in accomplishing the given goal. Some researchers (Baker and Paolucci, 1971; Foa and Foa, 1973) have suggested that the patterning of resources relative to particular goals provides a qualitative measurement that is especially suitable for determining resource allocation toward social goals such as the quality of life and educability.

Planning—the intermeshing of decisions about resources, values, goals, and standards—results in predetermining *what is to be done, why, how, when, by whom*, and *using which resources*. It is a conscious and continuing mental activity that involves visualizing problems and alternative solutions. Coupled with previously established routines (discussed in Chapter 6) these "planning decisions" result in a commitment by the family to a course of action.

Plans can be used for achieving a particular goal at one point in time or they can be more general and be used over a period of time. They can be intangible, such as a "mental picture" of what is to be done, or tangible, expressed in written specifications of goals and measurements for judging their achievement. In any case, plans constitute the basis for the everyday behavior of families: facilitating actions or behaviors and adapting them to the everchanging environment. The adaptation takes place through continuous checking and adjusting of actions (goals) to standards.


## IMPLEMENTING DECISIONS

Implementing is the process of translating decisions into action. It includes the thinking and doing activities—with the emphasis on the doing. Implementing encompasses those activities that the family organization performs to *facilitate action*, such as, assigning and delegating tasks, guiding, supervising, or actually carrying out a task, and controlling the outcomes of action through continuous checking and adjusting.


### Facilitating

Everyday family living necessitates the ordering of people and resources so that the varied and complex activities can be accomplished. Researchers (Tasker, 1962; Nichols, 1966; Mumaw, 1967; Dale, 1968; Nichols and Berger, 1969) have identified patterns of ordering tasks in the household as well as the relationship of these patterns to participation of family members in carrying out tasks. The ability to involve family members in carrying out tasks seems to be related to the level of self-actualization of the home manager, the degree of initiative or self-direction allowed the task performer, as well as acceptance of the rationale (importance or reasons) for the task. Family members are both "doers" and "deciders." If family decisions are to be carried to action, family members need to be involved in the decision making. The degree of participation in the decision will determine the commitment of family members to initiating action and to sustaining the activity to completion. Action can be facilitated through a number of guiding and supervisory techniques: giving clear instructions, helping or sharing in the task, giving praise or support.

### Checking

If actions and behaviors are to meet standards and reflect family values, continuous checking is necessary. Checking is a means of controlling the situation and provides the basis for adjustment (see Figure 13). While the goal is being effectuated (tasks performed, behaviors enacted) comparisons can be made between "what is" and "what ought to be." Deviations and their causes can be identified.

### Adjusting

If a discrepancy exists between expectation and attainment, corrections can be made. The adjustments can involve working to bring the goal up to the expected standard, changing the goal and/or changing the standard. The kind of adjustment or change depends on the information and energy flows and feedback within the family organization system and between the family system and its various environments. Feedback, both positive and negative, (resulting in maintaining stability or in introducing change) occurs continuously. Feedback can be noted between the family system and the other systems as well as between processes and subprocesses within the family organization; that is, between planning and implementing or the subparts of either (see Figure 10).

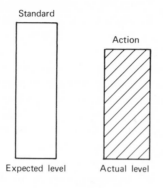

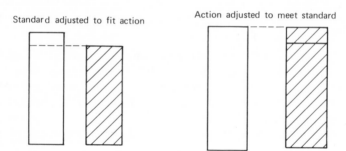

Figure 13. Comparison of Standard with Level of Goal Attainment

## SUMMARY

Managing resources, both human and nonhuman, is the central activity of the family organization. The processes of management—deciding and implementing actions—involve the entire family ecosystem: family members and those environments in which they are embedded and over which they have some measure of control. The processes themselves are always undergoing change, being modified, simplified, or elaborated. *How* the family organization manages resources determines its internal functioning and affects the environment that impinges on family members.

## SELECTED REFERENCES

Baerwaldt, Nancy A., and James N. Morgan. "Trends in Inter-family Transfers." In *Survey of Consumers 1971-72.* Lewis Mendel (ed.). Ann Arbor, Mich., Institute of Social Research, 1973.

Baker, Georgianne, and Beatrice Paolucci. "The Family as Environment for Educability in Costa Rica." *Journal of Home Economics* 63 (March 1971): 161-167.

Baker, Georgianne. "Patterning of Family Resources for Educability: Conceptualization and Measurement in Costa Rican Families." Unpublished Ph.D. dissertation, Michigan State University, 1970.

Bivens, Gordon. "The Grants Economy and the American Family" unpublished (mimeo.) Boulder, Colorado: Institute of Behavioral Science. 1975.

Boulding, Kenneth. *The Economy of Love and Fear.* San Francisco: Wadsworth Press, 1973.

Dale, Verda M. "An Exploration of the Relationship of Home Managers' Self-Actualization to Participation by Family Members in Home Activities." Unpublished Ph.D. dissertation, Michigan State University, 1968.

Diesing, Paul. *Reason in Society.* Urbana: University of Illinois Press, 1962.

Edwards, Kay P. "Goal-Oriented Behavior." *Journal of Home Economics.* 62 (1970): 652-655.

Fitcher, Joseph A. *Sociology.* Chicago: The University of Chicago Press, 1957.

Foa, Uriel G. "Interpersonal and Economic Resources." *Science* 171 (January 29, 1971): 345-351.

Foa, Uriel G., and Edna B. Foa. "Measuring Quality of Life: Can It Help Solve the Ecological Crisis?" *International Journal of Environmental Studies* 5 (1973): 21-26.

Foa, Uriel G., and Edna B. Foa. *Societal Structures of the Mind.* Springfield, Ill.: Charles C. Thomas Publisher, 1974.

Gross, Irma, E. Crandall, and M. Knoll. *Management in Modern Families.* New York: Appleton-Century-Crofts, 1973.

Maloch, Francille, and Ruth E. Deacon. "Proposed Framework for Home Management." *Journal of Home Economics.* 58 (1966): 31-35.

Mumaw, Catherine R. "Organizational Patterns of Homemakers Related to Selected Predispositional and Situational Characteristics." Unpublished Ph.D. dissertation, Pennsylvania State University, 1967.

Nichols, Addreen, and P. Berger. "Guiding Work of Teenage Girls." *Journal of Home Economics.* 61 (1969): 625-628.

Nichols, Addreen. "Organizational Processes Eliciting Help." *Journal of Home Economics.* 58: 727-728; 1966.

Paolucci, Beatrice, T. Faiola, and P. Thompson. *Personal Perspectives.* New York: McGraw-Hill, 1973.

Rescher, Nicholas. *Introduction to Value Theory.* Englewood Cliffs, N.J.: Prentice-Hall, 1969.

Rotter, Julian B. "External Control and Internal Control." *Psychology Today* 4 (June 1971): 37-42, 58-59.

Scanzoni, John. *Sexual Bargaining: Power Politics in the American Marriage.* Englewood Cliffs, N.J.: Prentice-Hall, 1972.

Tasker, Grace. "Case Studies of Homemakers Organization." Unpublished M.A. thesis, Cornell University, 1962.

Vickers, Geoffrey. *Value Systems and Social Process.* London, England: Pelican Books, 1970.

Waring, Ethel B. "Principles for Child Guidance" Ithaca, New York: Cornell University, Cornell Extension Bulletin 420, 1939.

Weick, Karl. "Group Processes, Family Processes, and Problem Solving." In Joan Aldous, Thomas Condon, Reuben Hill, Murray Straus, Irving Tallman (eds.) *Family Problem Solving.* Hinsdale, Illinois: The Dryden Press, 1971.

Wetters, Doris E. "Creative Aspects of Home Manager's Resourcefulness." Unpublished Ed.D. dissertation, Pennsylvania State University, 1970.

# Chapter 9
# Communication and the Management of Conflict

Communication is the systematic and patterned exchange of information that creates some level of shared experience and meaning among family members. It is essential to decision making and decision implementing. Because family members differ in their neural structure—needs, and experiences, they perceive environments differently. Hence a degree of incongruence in meanings among family members exists. This lack of completely congruent shared meanings results in conflict. Differences are mediated and conflict resolved among family members through transactions that bind family members together and result in decisions which simultaneously allow for individual action and group responses.

Families develop an interpersonal communication system in which each family member acts as a starter for the other person. One person transmits a sign or signal (message) in form of audible, visible, or tactical information and the other person responds by some action that triggers a response in the other. Satir (1972, pp. 113-114) points out that this ability of one person to perceive, receive, and respond to the messages of others is the factor that allows for change and diversity within the family. In open families there is an easy flow of information—each person is open to the messages of others; closed families are not able to perceive, receive, or respond to messages from one another readily—members close themselves off from one another.

A closed family provides for little or no change. It depends on edict and operates through force, both physical and psychological. The system evolves from the belief that people are basically evil and have to be controlled in order to be good. Relationships must be regulated with force; the person who has power knows the right way. Self-worth is secondary to power and performance. Change is resisted. On the other hand, an open system provides for change. Choices are offered. Self-worth is primary.

On the basis of comparisons made of troubled and nurturing families, Satir (1972, p. 4) concluded that troubled families displayed communication patterns that were growth impeding, unclear, vague, and indirect; rules were rigid, nonnegotiable, inhuman, and everlasting; interactions with other social systems were fearful, placating, and blaming; and self-worth was low. Nurturing families, on the other hand, had communication patterns that were growth producing, clear, specific, and direct; rules were flexible, humane, appropriate, and subject to change; interactions with other social systems were open and hopeful; and self-worth was high.

## COMMUNICATION WITHIN THE FAMILY

Communication involves both sending and receiving messages or information among family members. When the messages sent and received are similar, shared meaning results. In this case, communication is at a high level and uncertainty between persons is reduced. When a family member does not understand the message communication breaks down. Here expectations are not met and uncertainty, dissatisfaction, and conflict may occur. For example, Kevin was responsible for preparing supper. Marianne had suggested that he prepare hamburgers but she had not mentioned that she wanted the hamburger barbequed and so her secret expectation was not fulfilled. When Kevin prepared plain hamburgers, she refused to eat the meal. Many misunderstandings can be prevented if individuals are willing and take time to communicate their needs and ask for what they want.

To be able to send and receive messages honestly requires awareness and continued effort. When implementing family decisions, one person's behavior may be contingent upon that of another family member, so clear communication among family members is essential.

Clear communication depends on imparting information to others that expresses expectations from them as well as indications of how their behavior is being interpretated. Functional communication is stated clearly and honestly. The sender asks for feedback and is receptive to feedback when it is received. An individual who is frustrated by inability to communicate clearly may confuse matters still further by sending messages that are sarcastic, exaggerated, or foggy. According to Bach and Wyden (1968, p. 136), noncommunication tactics often cover up something that people are afraid to face openly, such as hostility, exploitative attitudes, overdependence, or fear of rejection.

The receiver of information can influence communication by ignoring a message, neutralizing its content, replying in terms of what the receiver thinks the sender expects, or trying to figure out the real meaning.

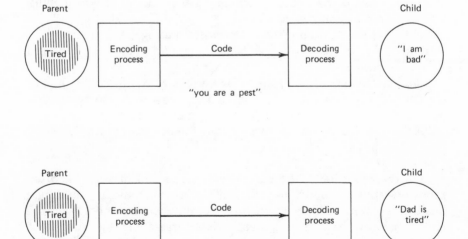

Figure 14. Differences Between A "You-message" and an "I-message" (From *Parent Effectiveness Training* by Thomas Gordon. Wyden Press, 1970.)

By the words selected for giving a message, particular responses are elicited. The sender of the message (encoder) selects specific words that are decoded by the receiver with a particular kind of orientation and hence trigger a response based on the receiver's perception of the sender's message. Gordon (1970, p. 117) has described one set of these messages as "you messages" and "I messages" (see Figure 14). A father who is tired must select a suitable code for letting the child know how he feels. If the father disguises his feeling and sends a "you message" that the child is pestering him, the message may be interpreted as meaning that the child is a bad person. When a parent's message to a child contains the word "you," the child is likely to feel blamed, rejected, resistant, or put down. In the following example Gordon illustrates a deteriorating relationship in which a "you message" sparked a conflict involving name-calling and reciprocal blaming:

Parent:   You're getting awfully irresponsible about doing your dishes after breakfast. ("you message.")

Child:    You don't always do yours every morning. ("you message.")

Parent:   That's different—Mother has lots of other things to do around the house, picking up after a bunch of messy children. ("you message.")

Child:    I haven't been messy. (Defensive message).

Parent:   You're just as bad as the others, and you know it. ("you message.")

Child:    You expect everyone to be perfect. ("you message.")

Parent:   Well, you certainly have a long way to go to reach that when it comes to picking up. ("you message.")

Child:    You're so darned fussy about the house. ("you message.") (p. 119)

On the other hand, the parent who uses an "I message" is often more effective in modifying the child's behavior and in building a healthier parent-child relationship. Communicating the effect the child's behavior has on the parent is less threatening than suggesting that the child is bad. The "I message" helps a child grow and assume responsibility. Gordon illustrated how active listening (hearing what the other person is saying) and the use of "I message" modified a parent's feeling, thus:

Father: I'm upset about the supper dishes being left in the sink. Didn't we agree that you would get them done right after dinner?

Jan: I felt so tired after dinner because I stayed up until three A.M. doing that term paper.

Father: You just didn't feel like doing the dishes right after dinner.

Jan: No. So I took a nap until ten thirty. I plan to do them before I go to bed. Okay?

Father: Okay by me. (p. 137)

### Dimensions of Communication

In their daily lives, family members become involved in making decisions based on information or messages that are both intellective and emotional. Egan (1970, pp. 141–189) has identified these dimensions of communication as pathos, logos, and poiesis. Some messages have a *pathos* base; they are rooted in feeling and emotion. Because many people find little emotional satisfaction in their work, they come home with intensified unmet needs. For example, one spouse's emotional frustration may interact with the other's intensified needs. Sometimes family members reduce tension by serving in community activities, thereby broadening the base of their emotional fulfillment. Others find less responsible solutions that may destroy family equilibrium: releasing tension by fighting in the home, extramarital adventures, emotional constriction, and vicarious emotional living. Suppressed emotion leads to ineffective communication which in turn leads to decreased productivity because meaning or understanding is not shared. Emotional awareness is enhanced when family members are open to experience and are able to perceive their environment.

*Logos* refers to the way a person translates thoughts into language. At times, a child surrenders the use of language because of parental disapproval, giving up hope of influencing others. Communication ceases and the child is impoverished because he has closed himself to messages. Some parents fear to communicate lest they involve themselves too deeply with others. Through language they impose limits on their world. Since language is filled with meanings for the person who is speaking, one can express identity through speech and is able to establish a high level of interpersonal relationships; deception and manipulation, which can indicate low levels of communication, may drive others away. Self-disclosure, clarity, content, and an invitation to respond encourage shared meaning.

The ability to be "poetic" in communicating—integrating verbal, nonverbal, and emotional expressions is a *poiesis* dimension. "In human dialogue, when words are meaningfully filled with human emotion, when feelings and emotions find creative expression in human language, the result is *poiesis.*" (Egan, 1970, p. 182) Meaningless words and unverbalized feelings hinder communication, a blending of the intellective and emotive dimension enriches communication and allows for greater flexibility in interpersonal relationships.

### Communication Networks

Just as the individual has a nervous system that receives and processes information, the family unit has a communication network. Katz and Kahn (1966, p. 237) identified three basic types of family networks as shown in Figure 15.

The *wheel* is a two-level hierarchy in which one family member is the primary decision maker. It may be the person who is most often at home to receive and transfer messages from the larger environment. The *circle* and *all-channel* networks are three-level hierarchies that allow more information exchange among the family members than does the two-level system. The circle and all-channel networks provide a greater potential of increasing information into the family; consequently, they may exhibit more characteristics of open systems than would be found in the wheel network unless, of course, the cen-

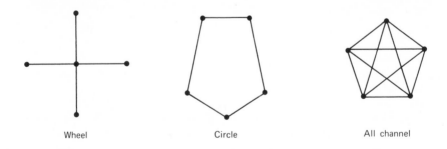

Wheel                    Circle                    All channel

Figure 15. Communication Networks (From *The Social Psychology of Organizations* by Daniel Katz and Robert L. Kahn. Copyright © 1966 by John Wiley & Sons.)

tral member of the wheel is especially receptive to new information. The all-channel network permits greater interaction among the family members than does the circle. At the same time, the all-channel network increases the possibility for noise interference in the system because of the number of communication links that are possible. The

|  | Open Family System | Closed Family System |
|---|---|---|
| *Noncrisis Situation* | | |
| Transaction patterns | Husband-wife balance between complementary and symmetrical, leaning toward symmetry | Husband-wife primarily complementary with husband in "one-up" position |
| | Parent-child transaction is complementary | Child in "one-down" position with father; symmetrical with mother |
| Interface | Flexible boundaries | Rigid boundaries |
| Communication | All-channel | Wheel |
| Feedback | Balance of positive and negative | Negative |
| *Crisis Situation (Wife Working)* | | |
| Transaction patterns | Husband-wife transaction becomes much more symmetrical, to the point of being competitive | Husband still "one-up" and wife resents more than previously |
| Interface | Additional boundaries across which information is transmitted; positive feedback into system | Additional boundaries present which husband chooses to ignore |
| Communication network | Still all-channel, with increased input from wife | Wheel becomes circular as wife adds dimension to network |
| Feedback | Temporarily positive feedback outweighs negative | Positive feedback introduced into system which closed system cannot cope with |

Figure 16. Hypothetical Open and Closed Family Systems. (From Nancy G. Harries, "A Systems Approach for Family Crisis Study." East Lansing: Unpublished paper, Michigan State University, 1970, pp. 19–21.)

time necessary to make decisions is increased in the all-channel network where each person can communicate with everyone else; yet the probability that a decision will be implemented is increased.

Harries (1970, pp. 18-21) illustrates the wheel and all-channel networks by viewing two families. Both family units functioned relatively smoothly in a noncrisis situation, although one family tended to be open to change and the other closed. She viewed both families before and after a hypothetical crisis that occurred when the wife (and mother of one child) began to work outside the home (see Figure 16). In both families, the women were trained professionally but neither had worked since marriage; both women had worked prior to marriage. When the child was old enough for nursery school, both women went back to work for added income. The woman in the open system family was more anxious to return to the professional world than the one in the closed family. Both husbands encouraged their wives to work because family expenses were mounting. A state of disorganization was introduced in both families as a result of the changes that took place when the wife began working. Because one family is open and the other closed, each will cope with crisis differently.

## NATURE OF CONFLICT

Conflict occurs when messages between persons are misinterpreted, when desires are not shared, or when perceptions differ and result in unexpected and uncertain responses. Conflict is a potent force that is abused and too often misunderstood. Family conflict is neither good nor bad, but simply a fact of life. It exists in all families and may in fact be essential to family stability. It can be destructive—producing quarrels, fights, hostilities. When conflict becomes intense or frequent, a family may become emotionally disorganized and the relationship between two or more persons may disintegrate. In an effort to avert these possibilities, families sometimes try to keep peace and harmony at any cost and may become apathetic. A healthy tension of matching and rematching perceptions creates a more adaptive family unit; one that is open to new messages and is in continuous process of change and growth.

Families are held together by interlocking bonds that develop through family interaction. These interactions occur through communication in the shared major task interdependencies and many minor collaborations. Bonds can be developed through identification and response of one person to another. These identity bonds reinforce or improve the self-concepts of family members. Bonds based on *identification* with another person who possesses admirable qualities link persons because of their shared or complementary qualities. The response evokes the kind of self-image an individual seeks to establish. Potentially, qualities of other individuals could be as gratifying as these. On the other hand, bonds that develop through interaction (crescive bonds) are uniquely irreplaceable. The development of bonds is the source of stability in the family; each person becomes indispensable to the other and the family members are locked into a continuing relationship (Turner, 1970, pp. 55-89).

Bonding is rooted in both conflict and harmony. Conflict does not exist in the family unless there are bonds that maintain interaction between antagonistic family members. Something must make the participants want to stay together or they would not be fighting over their differences; they would simply avoid each other. The family is a group in motion. Each decision situation calls for the family to interact in some manner. The immediate effect of a decision is less important than its contribution to cumulative family development. A decision that is reached easily but with resentment on the part of one family member may cause a later decision to proceed less smoothly.

A family may be highly efficient in making decisions and getting tasks done even though it experiences much conflict. Likewise, a harmonious family may have great difficulty reaching decisions. Turner (1970, p. 97) summarizes this relationship by saying that decision making is central to the accomplishment of group tasks; both conflict and harmony are central to the relationships among the family members.

Conflict can have constructive effects for individuals and families who learn to manage it. In fact, conflict may be an incentive toward greater activity to improve a situation. Creative management of conflict can provide flexible and manageable alternatives rather than letting the family get bogged down in continuing hostility and misunderstanding.

Conflict often results from verbal or conceptual misunderstandings rather than from incompatible values and goals. At other times conflicts can be attributed to mutually exclusive and incompatible goals held by two or more family members. The cost theory is applicable in such situations—selection of one desirable goal would be made at the expense of another desirable goal. Most conflicts probably are of the mixed-motive type in which the consequence most desired by one person is not the one most desired by the other.

A conflict is not resolved fully until the issue that caused it is either resolved or dead. Highly prized values that do not yield to accommodation are involved in deep-seated conflict. Tension from unresolved conflicts can build up within an individual and may eventually break out in overt conflict.

Conflict management begins with an understanding of the parties involved, since it is a function of individual behavior. Then the unresolved issue must be indentified—sometimes the real issue is hidden. The dynamics of the conflict situation include how each person responds to what he or she believes is the other's position and ways each manipulates the other's responses so as to reach at least a minimum agreement.

### Power

As a social group, every family is an organization of power, and many family acts are exercises in power. Power influences the decision process. The performance of its function by any part of the system affects the conditions under which other parts carry out their functions. Power can be used to block some action or it can mobilize resources toward a collective action. It can encourage compliance or impose sanctions.

Power refers to the degree to which one person achieves desired goals in spite of the resistance of another. In the family one person may effect change in another's activity or belief. Potentially, one member of the family could influence the selection and attainment of goals for the entire family. Power is judged strictly in terms of that one social system. For example, a father may have the kind of job where he feels "pushed around" and is never given a chance to express himself, yet he is domineering in his own home.

The distribution of resources may determine the power structure in the family. Imagine the power Mr. Masters had in his family as the only one who received a paycheck. His wife and children had to ask him for any money they needed. They were afraid to ask for things they wanted but didn't really "need." When the oldest daughter obtained her first job, her entire check was given each month to the father who returned a small allowance to her. In contrast, Mr. Hale chose to let the family help decide on the distribution of income. Each of the children received an allowance and understood what it was to cover. When Robert had an unusual opportunity to go with his class to the state capital, he felt free to discuss this with his father and work out arrangements to cover the cost of the trip. When the oldest daughter obtained her first job and was still living at home, she contributed to her parents a reasonable amount to cover her room and board but the rest of her pay check was hers. Power and influence are not synonymous. Mr. Hale probably had a great deal of influence on his family in helping them to understand the value of money and how to reach their goals. Mr. Masters had absolute power or control over his family; his influence may have helped the family learn how to handle money or it may have caused hostility or rebellion.

One person may have the power to determine the decision in many situations. If other members of the family have different preferences, this individual exercises power. For example, a dictatorial father might decide where the family will spend Sunday afternoons. In most family situations one person does not usually have sufficient power to control all the decisions nor is the power equally divided among all the family members. Power is diffused among the members of the family so that some have a great deal, others have a moderate amount, and some have very little. The distribution of power is likely to be imprecisely defined. The actual distribution is probably less important than an individual's perception of his or her power in relation to the others' power. A person acts in accordance with this apparent relative power, regardless of whether it is real. This is known as the *perception of strength theory.*

A high-power person can probably exert influence without making overt behavioral attempts to influence another. The high-power person initiates a number of communications and is successful in many attempts to influence but is less likely to be affected by the efforts of others to influence him or her. The person of low power is likely to behave deferentially toward high-power persons and to be suspicious of high-power persons who can withhold important resources.

Clark (1968, p. 354) summarizes some strategies for using power in influencing people: persuasion by using facts or reputation, inducement with favors or material rewards, invoking obligation or appealing to commitments, structuring behavior alternatives open to the others (usually by ignoring other possibilities), manipulating the perception of the alternatives by emphasizing certain aspects, diverting the other's attention by raising irrelevant issues to preclude taking the unwanted action, and coercion (threatening or actually applying force and violence). Some techniques are quite obvious while others are subtle. Misuse of power creates, rather than solves, family problems.

### Coalition

In some conflict situations, two or more family members form a coalition in which they cooperate with each other to achieve superior power and influence the outcome. They are in competition with other members of the family. The alliance of factions is, in general, temporary. As various issues arise, unions may be formed with different members of the family. The family is a complex interacting system and becomes even more so when coalitions are formed between members of the system. The power of an individual family member may depend on being involved in a winning coalition.

The determination of a child's allowance is a situation in which parents sometimes practice coalition. Before discussing a specific sum with the child, the parents may agree on an amount so they can present a united front. Likewise, siblings may band together to strengthen their demand that parents let them stay out later at night. When entering into a coalition, each person seeks the cheapest and most promising coalition. Entering a coalition costs an individual something. Since each participant has to concede something, the idea is to join with others whose views differ only slightly from yours or whom you could prevail upon to adopt your position. Each participant relinquishes freedom to take an individual position and pursue it; therefore, a coalition would be preferred in which that individual's power would be relatively high. The risk of indebtedness, which is incurred when some members of the coalition make greater concessions than others, is minimized by joining a coalition in which the benefits are fairly equal and no obligation for the future is likely to be imposed (Turner, 1970, pp. 128–130).

## CONFLICT RESOLUTION

Turner defines decision making as a "process directed toward securing unambivalent group assent and commitment to a course of action or inaction." (1970, p. 133) Family decisions are of three kinds. In *consensual* decisions all participants believe that the best decision was reached, and commitment to carrying it out is complete. Commitment is conditional when decisions are reached by *accommodation* because individuals assent to a proposal they do not privately think is best. An accommodation decision is always subject to being reopened in the midst of some future action. Individuals most closely in accord with the group decision may tend to be viewed as dominant; they are winners and the others are losers. *De facto* decisions are forced on a family by events that may prevent discussion or as an outcome of fruitless debate.

Ideally, the family will learn to manage conflict so that each person achieves some desires and grows through the process of arriving at the solution. Several techniques that have been used successfully in therapy or in business negotiations might be useful in resolving family conflicts.

### Assertiveness Training

A side-effect of early social training by parents is that many children lose much of their natural assertiveness. As adults they are unable to deal with others who try to manipulate them. Two basic principles of behavior modification are used in assertiveness training: "I can't be responsible for the other"; "I must be responsible for myself." One technique to meet manipulation is the "broken record," repeating the same thing over and over in a calm voice as a way of breaking through resistance. Suppose Mr. Taylor repeatedly criticizes his wife for being late with dinner. To each remark he made she could answer: "I am sorry I was late but I was doing something that was really important to me." Another approach, useful in handling unjustified criticism is "fogging"—agreeing in principle but not with the specific. For instance, Anthony's wife kept nagging him about looking for a job. His direct response was: "I feel like I am being nagged and I don't like to be nagged. Stop nagging me." When Julia failed to hear him, he tried the passive resistant "fog," simply agreeing with what she said: "You may be right." "I should get a job." "Perhaps you have a point." "I guess I do do that" (Smith, 1975).

A technique that can be used to disarm anger is to acknowledge that the individual is angry but refuse to talk about the issue until the person calms down. Another technique helps when an individual recognizes having made a mistake but another family member tries to make that person feel guilty. The key is to separate the two issues and respond to both (e.g., Elsie is scolding her husband, Jim, for not making reservations for their Christmas trip. Elsie says he is childish and irresponsible. Jim replies: "Yes, I forgot to make the reservations, but I will make them the first thing Monday morning. No, I am not a child."

### Constructive Aggression

Bach and Wyden (1968) have developed a theory of constructive aggression or fighting fairly in love and marriage. The aim is to reduce "self-and-other-defeating ways of coping . . . by maximizing intimacy-generating styles of aggression and minimizing hurtful and alienating hostility" (p. 329). Many marriages eventually end in separation, divorce, or marital counseling because couples brushed aside their marital troubles. Fight-phobic couples are particularly prone to finding escapes through overindulgence. "Conflict-habituated" couples engage in hostility rituals but do not display their conflicts to others because of their commitment to social-economic conveniences. On the other hand, true intimates keep their arguments current and specific. Their fights are not redundant and ritualized.

A technique of scoring intimate fights helps a couple to see that "only a joint win or loss is possible: either the partnership gains and emerges in an improved state as a result of an aggressive encounter or the unit loses and its relationship deteriorates" (Bach and Wyden, 1968, p. 159). The plus side of a fight profile includes dimensions of (1) reality, (2) injury kept within capacity of opponent to absorb it, (3) involvement of both persons, (4) assuming of responsibility by fight initiator, (5) humor, (6) overt expressions of aggression, (7) open communication, (8) focus on the here-and-now, and (9) attacks limited to specific observable behavior.

Each fight is analyzed also on an effects-of-fight profile. These effects include: (1) hurt, (2) new information, (3) control or power,

(4) fear, (5) trust, (6) revenge, (7) reparation, (8) autonomy, (9) catharsis, (10) cohesion, and (11) affection (Bach and Wyden, 1968, pp. 160–166).

### Negotiation

Every desire that demands satisfaction has the potential for triggering the negotiating process. Nierenberg (1973, p. 3) illustrates this by the action of his two sons arguing about which one would have the large slice of some leftover apple pie. Neither would agree to an even split. He negotiated by suggesting that one son cut the pie any way he wished and the other son could choose the piece he wanted. Each felt this was a fair solution. In a successful negotiation everyone wins; each family member comes out with some needs satisfied.

Negotiation presupposes that *both* the negotiator and the opposer want something—they have some unsatisfied needs. Building on Maslow's hierarchy of basic needs (see Chapter 4), Nierenberg (1973, pp. 82-86) points out that it is not necessary for one need to be fully satisfied before the next need takes over. Most people are partially satisfied in all of these needs. In seeking to satisfy their needs, people try to avoid physical discomfort (homeostatic needs), shun the unsafe (safety and security needs), appeal for understanding (love and belonging needs), abhor anonymity (need for esteem), dread boredom (need for self-actualization), fear the unknown (needs to know and understand), and hate disorder (esthetic need). The need theory gives a negotiator a wide variety of choice for affirmative or defensive use. Generally, a technique utilizing the more basic need will be more successful.

Nierenberg (1973, pp. 91-95) has identified six varieties of applications. The order of listing these varieties corresponds to the amount of positive control a negotiator ordinarily has in a particular situation. For example, the negotiator has more control over *his* working for the opposer's needs (variety 1) than letting the opposer work for his own needs (variety 2) and so on down to variety 6, which is least controllable (see Table 4). A few definitive words help suggest the kinds of action family members sometimes take in attempting to resolve problems.

Among the strategies that are designed to help in a negotiation is a proper sense of timing—knowing *when* to withhold anger, act impetuously, be silent, stop, alter the tone of voice, restrict the subjects

Table 4
Negotiation in Family Situations

| Situation | Need | Variety of Application |
|---|---|---|
| A mother (N*) persuades her would-be-suicide daughter (O*) to preserve her own life. | Homeostatic | (1) Negotiator works for opposer's needs. |
| A child (N) holds his breath to force his mother (O) to give in to his desires. | Homeostatic | (4) Negotiator works against his needs |
| A child (N) dares his sister (O) to do a dangerous act. | Safety and security | (5) Negotiator works against opposer's needs |
| Two teenage drivers (N and O), starting a distance apart, drive their cars rapidly toward each other. | Safety and security | (6) Negotiator works against opposer's and his own needs |
| A real estate broker creates a feeling of belonging between the seller (N) and buyer (O) by telling each all the nice things the other said. | Love and belonging | (3) Negotiator works for the opposer's and his own needs |
| A potential buyer (N) of a house calls attention to defective plumbing, bad roof, or other faults feeling that the owner (O) will give up his need for belonging with regard to the house for sale. | Love and belonging | (5) Negotiator works against opposer's needs |
| A husband (N) allows his errant wife (O) to sue him for divorce. He protects her reputation and she is forced to work for her need for public esteem by offering him a better property settlement, custody arrangements, etc. | Esteem | (2) Negotiator lets the opposer work for his needs |
| A father (N) teaches his son (O) the family business by starting him at the bottom. He works against the son's need for esteem so the son can acquire a full understanding of the business. | Esteem | (5) Negotiator works against the opposer's needs |

| | | |
|---|---|---|
| A wife (N) tells her husband (O) that he can be boss. She is playing on his need for self-actualization, his inner need to be manly. | Self-actualization | (1) Negotiator works for opposer's needs |
| A father (N) offers his son (O) a tough job that is difficult to accomplish, rather than an easy assignment. Assuming that the son accomplishes it successfully, he will gain great satisfaction. | Self-actualization | (2) Negotiator lets the opposer work for his needs |
| When a husband (O) is unfaithful to his wife (N), the signs may be obvious. She may decide to remain quiet and pretend to misunderstand what she sees rather than ask questions and provoke an unpleasant negotiation. She gives up her need to know and tries to improve her marriage in more subtle ways. | To know and understand | (4) Negotiator works against his needs |
| A husband (N) and wife (O) have been invited to a party and they disagree on whether to accept. They leave the outcome to the flip of a coin, acting against their need to know and understand. | To know and understand | (6) Negotiator works against the opposer's and his own needs |
| A couple (N) make an excessive demand when a prospective buyer (O) is interested in their motor boat. Then they offer to split the difference, working on the opposer's need for balance and symmetry. (This can be a dangerous tactic because too high an original demand will discourage further bargaining.) | Aesthetic | (1) Negotiator works for opposer's needs |
| A couple (N and O) are redecorating their house. They become impatient and sacrifice their aesthetic need just to get the work finished. | Aesthetic | (4) Negotiator works against his needs |

*N: Negotiator; O: Opposer

to be discussed, or give the impression that there is more information than there really is. *How* and *where* strategies include such behaviors as enlisting others to act on behalf of the involved individual, introducing several matters into the discussion to make concessions on one and gain on another, and taking something bit by bit until eventually possession of the entire piece is obtained.

Some of these strategies can be used destructively in a family; family members must be alert to such possibilities. Bargaining and negotiating can be integrative ways of resolving conflicts within a family. The family members are motivated to find a course of action that best expresses the group's desires. Differences are not suppressed or compromised but are brought out and harmonized.

### "No–Lose" Method

Many families resolve their conflicts by "win-lose" methods. Essentially this is a way of resolving differences through mutual agreement. Since this method is useful between individuals who possess relatively equal power, it might be called a "no-power" method. No one wins and no one loses, yet the solution must be acceptable to both. Here is one description of this method.

> Parent and child encounter a conflict-of-needs situation. The parent asks the child to participate with him in a joint search for some solution acceptable to both. One or both may offer possible solutions. They critically evaluate them and eventually make a decision on a final solution acceptable to both. No selling of the other is required after the solution has been selected, because both have already accepted it. No power is required to force compliance, because neither is resisting the decision (Gordon, 1970, p. 196).

Gordon illustrates the effectiveness of this method in the familiar battle over the cleanliness and neatness of a child's room (p. 196):

Mother:Cindy, I'm sick and tired of nagging you about your room, and I'm sure you're tired of my getting on your back about it. Every once in awhile you clean it up, but mostly it's a mess and I'm mad. Let's try a new method I've learned in class. Let's see if we can find a solution we both will accept—one that will make us both happy. I don't want to make you clean your room and have you be unhappy with that, but I don't want to be embarrassed and uncomfortable and be mad at you either. How could we solve this problem once and for all? Will you try?

Cindy: Well, I'll try but I know I'll just end up having to keep it clean.

Mother: No. I am suggesting we find a solution that would definitely be acceptable to both, not just to me.

Cindy: Well, I've got an idea. You hate to cook but like cleaning and I hate cleaning and love to cook. And besides I want to learn more about cooking. What if I cook two dinners a week for you and Dad and me if you clean up my room once or twice a week.

Mother: Do you think that would work out—really?

Cindy: Yes, I'd really love it.

Mother: Okay, then let's give it a try. Are you also offering to do the dishes?

Cindy: Sure.

Mother: Okay. Maybe now your room will get cleaned according to my standards. After all, I'll be doing it myself.

Among the reasons given for the effectiveness of the "no-lose" method are these: (1) A person who participates in making the decision is motivated to carry out the solution; (2) solutions of a higher quality (more creative and effective) are likely to be produced than either person would have thought of alone; (3) the thinking skills of both individuals are being developed; (4) hostility is reduced and the relationship is strengthened; (5) very little enforcement is required; the individuals carry out their part of the agreement in appreciation for not being pressured to accept a solution in which they lose; (6) an attitude of respect for the needs of self and the other makes power unnecessary; consequently there is less need to acquire defensive, coping mechanisms such as resisting and rebelling, submissiveness and passive surrendering, withdrawal and escape, and counterattacking or cutting the other down to size; (7) the *real* problem is likely to be defined rather than just the initial "presenting" problem; (8) parents communicate to children that *their* needs are important and children can be trusted to be considerate of parental needs in return; and (9) therapeutic changes have been reported in children after their parents started using the "no-lose" method. Children have shown improved school grades, peer relationships, openness in expressing feelings, responsibility about homework, independence, self-confidence, disposition, and eating habits. These improvements were accompanied by decreased temper tantrums and hostility toward school.

The "divided sheet" method begins with the parents telling the children that they would like to try to find solutions to their conflicts which would be acceptable to all so no one loses. As problems are brought up, they will be listed in the left column if they involve behavior of the children that does not tangibly or concretely affect the parents even though it bothers them. The right column will contain conflicts about the behavior that do affect the parents. When the list is completed, the parents will not hassle the children about any problem in the left column, but some solution acceptable to all will be worked out for all the problems in the right column. The children are so amazed and delighted to have the problems at the left thrown out that they are more willing to negotiate and offer solutions to the other problems. For example, a problem that is the child's responsibility, not requiring mutual problem solving, is "how he spends his allowance." A problem that must be  solved is "how much he contributes to the work required around the house."

Gordon's Credo (1970, pp. 305–306) expresses a humanistic philosophy that parents may find useful in their relationships with children and others:

### A CREDO*
For my relationships with youth and others

You and I are in a relationship which I value and want to keep. Yet each of us is a separate person with his own unique needs and the right to try to meet those needs. I will try to be genuinely accepting of your behavior both when you are trying to meet your needs and when you are having problems meeting your needs.

When you share your problems, I will try to listen accept-

*Thomas Gordon. *Parent Effectiveness Training.* New York: Peter H. Wyden, Inc./Publisher, 1970, pp. 305–306.

ingly and understandingly in a way that will facilitate your finding your own solutions rather than depending upon mine. When you have a problem because my behavior is interfering with your meeting your needs, I encourage you to tell me openly and honestly how you are feeling. At those times, I will listen and then try to modify my behavior.

However, when your behavior interferes with my meeting my own needs, thus causing me to feel unaccepting of you, I will tell you as openly and honestly as I can exactly how I am feeling, trusting that you respect my needs enough to listen and then try to modify your behavior.

At those times when either of us cannot modify his behavior to meet the needs of the other, thus finding that we have a conflict-of-needs in our relationship, let us commit ourselves to resolve each such conflict without ever resorting to the use of either my power or yours to win at the expense of the other losing. I respect your needs, but I also must respect my own. Consequently, let us strive always to search for solutions to our inevitable conflicts that will be acceptable to both of us. In this way, your needs will be met, but so will mine—no one will lose, both will win.

As a result, you can continue to develop as a person through meeting your needs, but so can I. Our relationship can always be a healthy one because it will be mutually satisfying. Thus, each of us can become what he is capable of being and we can continue to relate to each other in mutual respect, friendship, love and peace.

### Conjoint Family Therapy

Satir (1967) uses the approach of working with the entire family in a therapeutic setting, which helps them to grow in their relationships with each other. She stresses that the most important concept in therapy is *maturation*—a state in which the individual is fully in charge of self. "A mature person is one who . . . is able to make choices and decisions based on accurate perceptions about himself, others, and the context in which he finds himself; who acknowledges these choices and decisions as being his; and who accepts responsibility for their outcomes." The goal of conjoint family therapy is to help each member develop functional, mature patterns of behaving that enable each to deal in a competent and precise way with the world. A functional person will manifest self clearly to others; be in touch with internal signals as to thoughts and feelings; differentiate what is outside self; behave toward another person as a separate, unique self; treat differentness as an opportunity to explore rather than as a signal for conflict; deal with persons and situations in terms of "how it is" rather than wishes as to how it were; accept responsibility for what the individual feels, thinks, hears, and sees, rather than denying it; and openly negotiate the giving, receiving, and checking of meaning between self and others (Satir, 1967, pp. 91–92).

The family behaves as a unit. When a family identifies one member as a patient, that person's sickness may become essential to the family's stability as family members act together to achieve a balance. Satir indicates that "how they chose each other gives clues to why they may now be disappointed in each other. How they express their dissappointment with each other gives clues to why Johnny needs to have symptoms in order to hold the Jones family together" (Satir, 1967, pp. 6-7).

> **Example:** Ann and Don want to have dinner together. Ann wants chicken and Don wants hamburger. The place that serves hamburger does not serve chicken and vice versa.

Dysfunctional families handle such a disagreement by operating on the principle that "love and total agreement go together." They:

*Vacillate and postpone:* "Let's decide later what to eat." Sometimes they skip altogether.

*Try to coerce:* "We are going to eat hamburgers!"

*Try to delude each other:* "They are both food, so let's eat hamburger."

*Try to undermine each other:* "You don't *really* like chicken" or "You must be crazy to like chicken."

*Accuse and evaluate morally:* "You are bad and selfish for not wanting to eat hamburger. You never do what I want. You have mean intentions toward me."

In contrast, when "functional" people disagree, they may try:

*Coaxing:* "Please eat hamburgers."

*Taking turns:* "Let's eat chicken this time and hamburger next time."

*Finding an alternative that pleases both:* "We both like steak so let's eat steak." or "Let's find another restaurant which serves hamburger *and* chicken."

*Taking into account a realistic concern which outweighs their separate wishes:* "Since the hamburger place is nearer and we're in a hurry, let's eat hamburger."

*Balancing their separate wishes against their wish to be together:* "You eat hamburger since you like it so much and I will eat chicken, and I will see you later." (They are able to separate temporarily and find independent solutions when feasible.)

*Using a third person to make the decision for them* (as a last-ditch effort): "Charlie wants to eat with us. Let's ask Charlie where he wants to go" (Satir, 1967, p. 14).

## SUMMARY

Conflict, rooted in the differences in needs, demands, and perceptions that exist among family members and between the family and the environment, must be understood and managed for family decision making. Effective communication is essential to conflict resolution and the harmonious adaptation of family members to one another and to their environments. Improving communication in the family facilitates family decision making and makes more certain that the decisions will be carried out.

## SELECTED REFERENCES

Bach, George R., and Peter Wyden. *The Intimate Enemy.* New York: Avon Books, 1968.

Clark, Terry N. (ed.) *Community Structure and Decision-Making: Comparative Analyses.* San Francisco: Chandler Publishing Company, 1968.

Egan, Gerard. *Encounter: Group Processes for Interpersonal Growth.* Belmont, Calif.: Brooks/Cole Publishing Company, 1970.

Gordon, Thomas. *Parent Effectiveness Training.* New York: Peter H. Wyden, 1970.

Harries, Nancy G. "A Systems Approach for Family Crisis Study." Unpublished paper, Michigan State University, 1970.

Katz, Daniel, and Robert L. Kahn. *The Social Psychology of Organizations.* New York: John Wiley & Sons, 1966.

Nierenberg, Gerard I. *Fundamentals of Negotiating.* New York: Hawthorn, 1973.

Satir, Virginia. *Conjoint Family Therapy.* (Revised edition.) Palo Alto: Science and Behavior Books, 1967.

Satir, Virginia. *Peoplemaking.* Palo Alto: Science and Behavior Books, 1972.

Smith, Manuel J. *When I Say No, I Feel Guilty.* New York: Dial Press, 1974.

Turner, Ralph H. *Family Interaction.* New York: John Wiley & Sons, 1970.

# Chapter 10
## Effects of Family Decisions on Humanity

How do choices made in the family ecosystem affect the future of humankind? How can these effects be identified, assessed, and consciously directed? What rights and responsibilities does a particular family have regarding the use of the limited resources of the world environment? These, and other, serious questions must be posed and addressed by all families now and in the future.

Decisions made in *every* family, whether informed and deliberate or uninformed and semiconscious, affect humanity. Families are inextricably tied one to another and to environments in an ever-widening web of transactions. What happens in one family makes a difference not only to that family, but to others as well, for families are dependent on one another and on the resources of the natural environment. In turn, environments respond and change depending on how families function within them, thus environments become more or less supportive of human development.

Family ecosystems are in a continuous process of seeking equilibrium. The ability of the family to make decisions that change or elaborate its own internal functioning and structure in response to

173

demands from varied and complex environments is a measure of its adaptibility, and families differ from one another and over time in adaptive capability. Particular family ecosystems are unique; hence, their decisions are unique. The processes, however, of managing (deciding and implementing actions) for adaptation are universal. The family organization may at times make decisions that work toward preserving or maintaining the family in a given state; that is, keeping things "as is." At other times it will make decisions that will bring about change and innovation within its own structure. One family may initially confront environmental conditions similar to those of the family next door, yet end up having attained quite dissimilar values and goals. The outcomes will vary because of the kinds of choices each family makes. Although environmental conditions may be similar, each family may perceive the information or messages from the environment differently and its particular goals may also differ; hence its actions and the goals it reaches may differ. On the other hand, families may live in quite different environments, the conditions of everyday living may be very diverse from the stance of specific resources and demands such as food, money, or paid work opportunities yet they may end up having attained similar levels and standards of living. The content of decision making in families may differ, both in terms of input and output, yet the processes of systemic seeking of equilibrium or harmonious adaptation remain essentially the same.

The kinds of decisions they make in response to environmental impacts determines what happens to the family unit, to each family member, and to the environment. This continuous adaptation—action, response, reaction—affects both people and environments. It is these processes of family decision making and decision implementing that shape the destiny of families. At issue at all times is the responsibility families have for making decisions that will assure optimum development for family members now and in future generations. Each of us must take time to reflect on the effects of particular family choices on humanity. The effects of family decisions on humanity can be evaluated in some measure by examining two areas of choice in family ecosystems: consumption and socialization.

## CONSUMPTION

The family organization, in the strict sense of the word, is a consuming unit. It organizes and orders the activities of family members for taking basic resources from the natural environment and utilizing them. In a more popular sense, the family can also be viewed as a production unit because it transforms resources into useful forms for consumption. For example, food is transformed from raw to cooked form and assembled, combined, and ordered to produce meals for family consumption. The multitudinous decisions that the family organization makes in order to transform resources from the environment to useful forms for the family's satisfaction are illustrative of consumption choices. The possibilities for making consumption decisions are constrained or enhanced by the availability of resources in the environment. Consumption decisions determine the level and quality of day-to-day family living. Without adequate resources, both the level and quality of living can be diminished.

As consumers, families are linked to their environment. For example, adequate food must be supplied by the environment. The quality of food that is produced is affected by the air, water, and soil in which it grows. Family decisions can develop or destroy nutritious food resources. The family whose car burns excessive oil is contributing to air pollution, which can affect the growth of plants and animals. The family who operates the air conditioning unit at all times, even when windows are open, is wasting a scarce resource that may be needed to provide for the growth of wheat as well as for direct human services. Family members who view their decisions as small and insignificant are forgetting the combined impact of many families living within the confines of the earth's ecosystem. To waste food, as is done in some families and societies, is a luxury not many can or should tolerate. Families who accept a responsible consumer role make decisions about products carefully. They are cognizant of the interdependence of family and environment. Decisions are based on knowing what the resources from the environment are; the costs of transforming and using resources; what the effects of these transformations are likely to be on the family itself; and what effects the family consumption activities will have on the environment. For example, what kinds of wastes will the family put into the environment? Can these wastes be recycled? What kind of benefits to larger social and economic systems ensue from the family? What share of the world's finite energy resources are used by a given pattern of eating or shelter?

It is difficult to measure the level of adaptation, that is, how family-environment interactions and transactions influence the ecosystem. Although difficult, measuring level of adaptability is essential to prudent decision making.

Levels of adaptability need to be determined quantitatively, qualitatively, and relative to the overall balance of family-environment. Fritsch and Castleman (1974) have developed a quantitative measure that makes it possible for households to determine their expenditures of limited natural resources, especially fossil fuels, and to compare their expenditures with those of households internationally. This life style index makes it possible to quantify energy transformation expenditures of the household, such as energy units expended in: "a) household heating, cooling, and lighting; b) foodstuffs—production, freight, processing, packaging, retailing; c) consumer products and leisure activities; d) transportation; e) social and . . . government" (Fritsch and Castleman, 1974, p. 3). Knowing the quantity of energy (resources) expended is one aspect of assessing the level of adaptability. When a family can determine quantitatively how much of a resource it is using compared to what is available now and in the predictable future it is in a better position to make decisions. Quantitative dimensions of energy use would need to include dimensions of by-products that result from using a particular type of resource and whether or not the resource was renewable.

Knowing *how much* energy is used is not informative, however, of the quality of life that results from use. Qualitative dimensions of energy use by families would need to include the degree to which family values were mediated and goals attained. The satisfactions realized by the family are dependent on the quality of the environment. Such aesthetic amenities as land designated for parks, streams, wildlife; reductions in congestion and noise; pleasing architecture all enhance the potential for realizing values of health and beauty. (See Chapter 8 for further discussion.)

Measures of levels of adaptability of family to larger social systems may provide a base for determining the structure and form of the social organization that can best create and transform different resources (Foa and Foa, 1973). An important by-product may be a decrease in the demand for those goods and services that are spurred by unsatisfied particularistic needs. This will reduce pollution and the consumption of energy. Quantifying resource expenditures can be helpful in understanding the critical balance between family and environment and provide insights into the effects of family consumer choices on both the survival of humans and the maintenance of an environment that supports and enhances human existence.

Accelerating depletion of energy reserves and environmental pollution resulting from rising consumption levels coupled with increases in human population may tip the human system-environment balance, resulting in an environment that is increasingly hostile to human survival. It has been suggested that improvement of the social environment and especially of the intimate family ecosystem "will reduce the threat to the physical environment caused by excessive demands for material resources . . . . The following six classes of resources appear necessary and sufficient to account for basic needs of human beings: love; status; information; money; goods; and services . . . . All six classes of resources contribute to the quality of life, so that when any of them falls below a minimum level, quality of life is impaired" (Foa and Foa, 1973, pp. 21, 23).

Work is underway in developing indicators that will measure both the quantity and quality of resources created and used in various environments including the family. Ways of determining the costs and benefits of any given option with regard to both human life and the environment are necessary. Such questions as these need to be posed: What is the cost to the individual and family or to other social systems and the natural environment when the human resource is developed in a universalistic rather than particularistic setting (e.g., an institutionalized setting, such as infant care center, rather than the particularistic, intimate setting of family)? Is the family or a social institution better able to develop some resources (i.e., trust, love, values and attitudes, decision-making skills)? If denied love, does one choose material goods as a substitute?

The web of interdependencies of people to environments can become ever more apparent as one examines the processes of decision making in the family ecosystem. Family decisions do affect environments; environments can modify the structure and form of all social systems including the family.

## SOCIALIZATION

A primary task of the family organization is that of socializing its members, especially children. "The young human animal must acquire an immense amount of traditional knowledge and skill and must learn to subject his inborn impulses to the many disciplines prescribed by his culture, before he can assume his place as an adult member of society." (Murdock, 1949, p. 10) Socialization in the family is influenced by information inputs from the environment; including demands, values, and needs. These are perceived and interpreted by the family organization. Through processes of communication, interaction, and transactions among family members, decisions about appropriate ways of behaving are made.

The family provides a pervasive setting that enables a child to develop understanding and mastery of the environment. As a child grows, the family not only guides development but also serves as a model for behavior within and outside the family group. The decisions that families make to reduce tension and resolve conflict among family members not only determine the stability and harmony of the family unit, but also determine the degree to which basic needs are met. Family members are encouraged to either express or repress emotions by the way social decisions are made in the family. The long-lasting and far-reaching effects of repressing emotions in the family are described vividly by Branden (1971, p. 26):

A person denies his need to find human beings he can respect, admire, and love—and then superimposes on himself the unreal personality of a cynic. A person denies his loneliness—and then withdraws from people behind an artificial front of indifferent remoteness. A person denies his need of self-esteem—and then proceeds to seek it in the bodies of an endless procession of women. A person denies his longing for beauty—and then affects a vulgarity aimed at proving his "practicality" and "realism". A person denies his pain—and then loses his sensitivity and buries his perceptiveness beneath a brutal blindness to the pain of others, including those he professes to love. A person denies his anxiety— and then finds himself locked in a self-made tomb of passive rigidity. A person makes himself thoroughly invisible—and then agonizes over the fact that no one sees or understands him. A person extinguishes one part of his personality after another— and then feels horror when he looks inward and finds only a sterile void.*

Blindness concerning important aspects of self develops through

*From *The Disowned Self* © 1971 by Nathaniel Branden with permission of Nash Publishing Corp.

selective perception of information and is reinforced by experiences within the family. This can lead to a blindness or misreading of important aspects of the environment, hence causing one to become oblivious to or act contrary to opportunities offered by the environment.

How do socialization decisions affect humanity? How does the environment modify interpersonal relations and make possible the achievement of goals? Again, the need to discern the level of adaptation, both quantitatively and qualitatively, becomes apparent.

An Index of Resourcefulness of the family ecosystem as it relates to the societal goal of educability of the preschool child was developed by Baker (1970, p. 10). The index is comprised of quantitative and qualitative dimensions of *resources available* in the family environment and the quantitative and qualitative dimensions of *resources used* by the child (see Table 5).

Family resourcefulness is measured by computing separate resource scores, transforming these into ratings and summarizing them as high, middle, and low levels of relation of resources to educability. Environments for educability of children in Costa Rica varied from low to moderately powerful and pervasive. "The pattern of resources is shown to be neither completely supportive nor consistently negative in relation to the suggested goal. Environmental effects upon the child might possibly be controlled or at least mediated by improvement in family status levels, by direct efforts in relation to low and moderately rated resource categories, or by efforts . . . totally outside of the family, or by a combination of all methods" (Baker and Paolucci, 1971, p. 166). The kinds of decisions families make relative to resources determine the level of attainment of both familial and social goals. The level of attainment of the goal of educability does have impact on the larger social and economic environment in which the child functions and has future implications in how options for the child will be expanded or constrained. These effects will permeate not only the given family organization and related social and economic environments but also the future family and individuals with whom the child will interact! The environment influences family members and, in part, structures the interpersonal relationships in and out of the family and, through these relationships, it influences the achievement of some family, personal, and social goals.

**Table 5**
Summary definitions of Dimensions by Resource Categories.

| Resource Category | Availability-Quantity (AQN) | Availability-Quality (AQL) | Use-Quantity (UQN) | Use-Quality (UQL) |
|---|---|---|---|---|
| Space | Household spaces in relation to persons | Variety in housing elements | Child's usual activities involving spaces and objects in household | Relation of child's activities to future school success |
| Child's movement | Movement-related elements in household, neighborhood, or community | Restriction of elements to household | Child's actions involving movement elements | Relation of child's movement to future school success |
| Care and appearance | Food and clothing items | Regularity of routine in care and appearance | Child's usual clothing and food consumption | Relation of child's care and appearance activities to future school success |
| Child's play | Play objects and activities | Variety of objects and activities | Child's usual play | Relation of child's play to future school success |
| Child's tasks and work | Possibilities for personal tasks and work | Involvement of family in child's tasks and work | Child's usual participation in tasks and work | Relation of child's tasks and work to future school success |
| Child's learning | Objects and activities for learning | Involvement of family in child's learning | Child's usual participation in learning | Relation of child's learning activities to future school success |

| Family learning | Objects and activities for learning | School-relatedness of family learning activities | Family's usual participation in learning | Relation of family's learning activities to child's future school success |
| Child's contacts | Contacts and social activities | Centered within the family | Child's usual contacts and social activities | Relation of child's contacts and activities to future school success |
| Family contacts | Contacts and social activities | Centered within the family | Family's usual contacts and social activities | Relation of family's contacts and social activities to child's future school success |

Source: Georgianne Baker. "Patterning of Family Resources: Conceptualization and Measurement in Costa Rican Families." Unpublished Ph.D. dissertation, Michigan State University, 1970, p. 10.

## INTERDEPENDENCE OF FAMILY (PRIVATE) AND SOCIETAL (PUBLIC) DECISIONS

Each day families make a number of decisions that are enacted in behaviors that are either satisfying or disappointing to the family unit or to individual members. These choices feed directly into the physical and social environments that surround the family. The private choices of the family have an impact on the larger society and on public decisions. For example, families reshape society by the number of children they decide to have, the consumer choices they make, and the votes they cast in support or rejection of particular social goals. A family might decide to support legislation that benefits families. Families can become involved in programs that protect consumers, improve nutritional status and education, provide health care services, support equal opportunities in marriage and employment, protect public health and safety in housing, promote voluntary control of population and responsible parenthood, control environmental pollution, and provide family life and sex education programs. Family members can seek information on proposed legislation pertaining to certain topics. They can express their viewpoints by writing, visiting, or telephoning their legislators. They can share their opinions, lead public interest groups, enlist the support of voluntary and government agencies, and collaborate with others to gain strength in bringing about needed changes. They can testify at public hearings to proclaim humanistic values and concerns for the aged and the young. They can write to regulatory agencies for information on citizens' rights and responsibilities and to prod agencies to enforce their standards. If a company in their community is polluting the environment, the family can buy a share of stock in that company and gain the right to raise questions at the annual meeting—or they can boycott the products of the company. In innumerable ways families can influence public decisions and help determine public policy.

Some of the problems that are affecting society are: population growth and concentration, environmental pollution, poverty, crime, drug abuse, racial enmity, inadequate housing, malnutrition, and urban blight. Each of these affect the family—and the family may contribute to the problem or solution by the kinds of decisions it has made or is making. These problems can be viewed as gaps between what people expect and the realities of a given social condition. The expectation-reality gap can be described as the disparity between what should be and what is in the society. Despite an astonishing gain in the real income of United States families in the lowest brackets during the 1960s, public expectations outraced realities and poverty was viewed as a serious problem at a time when its incidence had been reduced 60% from its 1947 level. The expectation-reality gap changes with time. It is based on information input from the environment, and this information is transformed in the family into a "reality" for it.

The family can play a key role in the dynamics of dissatisfaction, thereby influencing the expectation-reality gap. Expectations are shaped partly by the mass media. Family decisions determine which newspapers, magazines, radio and television programs will provide a flow of information into the home. Expectations are heavily influenced by publicly expressed views of political leaders. Through family discussions, family members can learn to evaluate propaganda and can lend support to candidates who seem to be most responsive in bringing about orderly social change. In addition, the family organization can be a stabilizing influence as members become confused, frustrated, or alienated from their government when it fails to hold social expectations within the boundaries of public resource constraints. By helping its members appreciate the realities of national achievement and by encouraging realism about social expectations, the family helps build national self-esteem.

Research (Andrews and Withey, 1974) has indicated that feelings about self, family, and family interaction, one's home, money, job, and concern with food and services are major factors in the overall perception of what constitutes "the good life." These feelings are translated as a quality of life; family members and the near environment of work and community are interdependent in shaping this view.

Probably men will always differ as to what constitutes the good life. They need not differ as to what is necessary for the long survival of man on earth. Assuming that this is our wish, the conditions are clear enough. As living beings we must come to terms with the environment about us, learning to get along with the liberal budget at our disposal, promoting rather than disrupting these great cycles of nature—of water movement, energy flow, and material transformation that have made life itself possible. As a physical goal we must seek to attain what I have called a steady state. The achievement of an efficient dynamic equilibrium between man and his environment must always, in itself, have the challenge and charm of an elusive goal (Sears, 1969, p. 401).*

The family organization plays a unique role in instigating change in the environment. Broderick (1976, p. 17) points out that "the shifts in birthrate over the last three generations, as dramatically as any other element, have contributed to changing public policy and economic fluctuations. And the brithrate, like other social statistics, is nothing more than the cumulation of individual family decisions." Increasingly, the kinds of questions raised by Augenstein (1969, p. 99): "What is the right thing to do?"; "What set of values do we use?"; and "Who should be making the decisions?" become the concern of individuals and families as the relationship of population to environment becomes more fragile.

How can families make decisions and structure activities to most closely approximate this elusive balance between human beings and nature? One way, we believe, is to use an ecological approach that places emphasis on viewing the family and environment holistically, allows one to note the interdependence of people to people, families to one another and to other social systems, and, especially, the interdependence of families to the natural environment.

The last chapter will be written by you, the reader, as you participate in the everyday decisions of the family and are confronted by the challenge and desire to seek the universal goal of harmonious adaptation, innovation, and change among families and environments.

## SELECTED REFERENCES

Andrews, Frank, and Stephen Withey. "Assessing the Quality of Life as People Experience It." Paper presented at American Sociological Association meeting, Montreal, 1974.

*From Paul B. Sears: "The Steady State" in Shepard and McKinley: THE SUBVERSIVE SCIENCE: ESSAYS TOWARD AN ECOLOGY OF MAN, 1969. Reprinted from *The Key Reporter.* Volume 24, number 2, Winter 1959. By permission of The United Chapters of Phi Beta Kappa.

Augenstein, Leroy. *Come, Let Us Play God.* New York: Harper and Row Publishers. 1969.

Baker, Georgianne. "Patterning of Family Resources for Educability: Conceptualization and Measurement in Costa Rican Families." Unpublished Ph.D. dissertation, Michigan State University, 1970.

Baker, Georgianne, and Beatrice Paolucci. "The Family as Environment for Educability in Costa Rica." *Journal of Home Economics* 63 (March 1971): 161-167.

Branden, Nathaniel. *The Disowned Self.* New York: Bantam Books, 1971.

Broderick, Carlfred B. "Roles, Family and Change." *Penney's Forum: New Perspectives on Changing Roles.* (Spring/Summer 1976.) New York: J. C. Penney Company. p. 17.

Foa, Uriel G., and Enda B. Foa. "Measuring Quality of Life: Can It Help Solve the Ecological Crisis?" *International Journal of Environmental Studies.* 5 (1973): 21-26.

Fritsch, Albert J., and Barry I. Castleman. *Lifestyle Index.* Washington, D.C.: Center for Science in the Public Interest, 1974.

Murdock, George. *Social Structure.* New York: The Free Press, 1949.

Sears, Paul B. "The Steady State: Physical Choice and Moral Law." In Paul Shepard and Daniel McKinley (eds.). *The Subversive Science: Essays Toward an Ecology of Man.* Boston: Houghton Mifflin Company, 1969.

# Index

Accommodation, 161
Adams, Richard N., 86, 89
Alderfer, Clayton P., 60-61, 72
Alienation, 40, 49-50, 75
Ames, Russell E., Jr., 127
Andrews, Frank, 183, 184
Anomie, 49-50
Assertiveness, 161-162
Auerswald, Edgar H., 21, 26
Augenstein, Leroy, 184, 185

Bach, George R., 151, 162-163, 171
Baerwaldt, Nancy A., 138, 147
Baker, Georgianne, 100, 111, 137, 144, 147, 179-181, 185
Balvin, Richard S., 51
Bean, Nancy M., 106, 111
Bengston, Vern L., 64, 72
Berger, P., 145, 147
Berlyne, D. E., 120, 121, 127
Bivens, Gordon, 138, 147
Blake, Judith, 79, 89
Blood, Robert O., 110, 111
Boulding, Kenneth, 138, 147
Branden, Nathaniel, 178, 185
Broderick, Carlfred B., 79, 89, 184, 185
Bronfenbrenner, Urie, 50, 51
Buckley, Walter, 24, 26
Bustrillos, Nena, 94, 95, 96, 97, 100, 111

Carza, Raymond T., 115, 127
Castleman, Barry I, 176, 185

Centers, Richard, 110, 111
Central satellite, 106-109
Centrifugal forces, 22
Centripetal forces, 22
Chain decisions, 12, 51, 70, 106-109, 130
Change, 7, 9, 50, 78-80
Children, 57, 68, 75, 77, 79
Clark, Terry N., 43, 51, 159, 171
Cognitive complexity, 118-121
Communication, 134-136, 149-156
Compton, Norma H., 19, 20, 26, 58, 72
Conflict, 8, 39, 77, 99, 102-104, 115, 120, 133, 156-171
Conjoint family therapy, 169-171
Constraints, 117
Consumer protection, 44
Control, 10-13, 56, 107, 128, 132
Cooper, W., 52
Crandall, E., 147
Culture, 46-48, 76-77, 136

Dale, Verda M., 145, 147
Davis, Allison, 47-48, 51
Deacon, Ruth E., 133, 147
Decidophobia, 12-14
Defense mechanisms, 55, 117, 167
Deprivation, 40, 62
Diamond, Florence R., 51
Diamond, Solomon, 46-47, 51
Diesing, Paul, 100, 111, 122, 127, 137, 147
Dissonance, 94

187

Dreikurs, Rudolf, 8, 14
Driver, Michael, 41, 52
Dyk, R. B., 73

Easen, Elmer, 78, 89
Economic decisions, 102, 104-105
Edens, Thomas, 52
Edwards, Kay P., 133, 147
Egan, Gerard, 153-154, 171
El-Assal, Mohammed M., 73
Elbing, Alvar O., Jr., 30, 31, 32, 33,
  52
Elements of decision making, 94
Emerick, Robert, 73
Energy, 86-88
Equifinality, 24-25
Exchange of resources, 137-143
Existence needs, 60-63, 71
Expectations, 8, 40, 76-78, 110, 145-
  146, 151, 182-183

Faiola, T., 148
Fate, 10-13, 56, 69, 115
Fatkvson, H. F., 73
Feedback, 74, 145, 151
Field dependent, 55
Fitcher, Joseph A., 129-147
Foa, Edna B., 140, 144, 147, 177,
  185
Foa, Uriel G., 139, 140-142, 144, 147,
  177, 185
Frankena, William, 75, 89
Freedom, 10-11, 82
Fritch, Albert J., 176, 185
Fromm, Erich, 49, 52
Future, 5, 12, 30, 51, 70, 95, 129,
  132, 142

Gans, Herbert J., 50-51, 52
Glass, David C., 100, 111
Goals, 54, 63, 76, 104-105, 129-133
Goodenough, D. L., 73
Gordon, Milton, 46, 47, 52
Gordon, Thomas, 151-153, 166-169,
  171
Government, 38, 44-46, 134, 138,
  182-183
Grants, 138
Graves, Clara W., 71, 72

Gray, Loren, 8, 14
Gross, Irma, 132, 135, 136, 147
Growth needs, 60-63

Habit, 97
Hall, Olive A., 19, 20, 26, 58, 72
Halliday, Jean, 100, 111
Harries, Nancy G., 96, 111, 155-156,
  171
Hazard, John I., 30, 52
Heer, D. M., 110, 111
Heuristic methods, 122
Hogan, M. Janice, 25, 26, 28, 52
Hook, Nancy C., 17, 26
Hoyt, Elizabeth E., 11, 14, 54, 72, 93,
  112

Immediate closure, 95-97
Indecision, 12-14, 65
Information processing, 96-97, 100,
  113-127, 132
Interdependence, 5, 17-18, 29, 46, 54,
  63, 88, 106, 173-184

Jacobson, Margaret, 68, 72

Kahn, Robert L., 154, 172
Kantor, David, 21, 26
Karlins, Marvin, 127
Karp, S. A., 73
Katz, Daniel, 154, 172
Kaufmann, Walter, 12-14
Kluckhohn, Florence R., 69, 72
Knoll, M., 147
Koenig, Herman, 28, 29, 52
Kohlberg, L., 68, 72
Kohn, Melvin, 42, 52
Komarovsky, Mirra, 110, 112
Kuhn, Alfred, 23, 24, 26, 93, 112

Lee, Dorothy, 47, 52
Lee, Wayne, 8, 14
Lehr, William, 21, 26
Levy, Charles S., 10, 14
Lexicographic ordering, 96-97
Linkage, see Chain decisions
Linton, Ralph, 63, 72
Lovejoy, Mary C., 64,
  72

McKinley, Daniel, 184, 185
Maloch, Francille, 133, 147
Maslow, Abraham H., 59, 72, 163
Maxim strategy, 124-125
Mejia-Pivaral, V., 111
Micklin, Michael, 17, 26
Miller, David W., 123, 127
Miller, James G., 116, 117, 127
Minimax strategy, 125-126
Minority groups, 56
Mobility, 50-51
Mode, 94-95
Morals, 67
Morgan, James N., 138, 147
Morphogenesis, 24
Morphostasis, 24
Motivation, 8, 10, 71, 76, 114-115, 136
Multifinality, 25
Mumaw, Catherine R., 145, 147
Murdock, George, 177, 185
Myers, Anna M., 106, 112

Needs, 58-63, 163
Negotiation, 163-166
Nichols, Adreen, 145, 147
Nierenberg, Gerard I., 163-166, 172
"No-Lose" method, 166-169
Nonprogrammed decisions, 97-99
Norms, 77

Objective elimination, 95-96
Odum, Eugene P., 15, 26
Olson, David H., 110, 112

Paolucci, Beatrice, 17, 25, 26, 28, 52, 99, 104, 106, 112, 133, 144, 147, 148, 179, 185
Parent-child relationship, 56, 64, 77, 79, 82-85
Past, effects of, 5, 12, 31, 49, 51, 59, 70, 95, 97, 114-115, 129
Perception, 54, 55-58, 63, 102, 114, 117-118, 120, 159, 179, 183
Personality, 55
Phares, Jacqueline, 127
Piaget, J., 68, 72
Plonk, Martha A., 106, 107, 108, 112
Policy decision, 107

Power, 43, 46, 110, 150, 158-160, 168-169
Preference ranking, 63, 95-97
Price, Dorothy, 100, 112
Pro and Con, 123-124
Programmed decisions, 97-99, 108

Rainwater, Lee, 110, 112
Rationality, 100, 107
Raven, Bertram H., 110, 111
Recinose, L., 111
Rescher, Nicholas, 63, 73, 129, 148
Resourcefulness, 137, 179
Resources, 19, 38, 71, 76, 86, 88, 105, 108, 131-133, 136-144, 175, 179
Rewards, 56
Risk, 9, 35, 98, 121-122
Rivlin, Alice M., 39, 52
Robopath, 49
Rokeach, Milton, 64, 73
Roles, 6, 12, 42, 76-80, 110
Roosevelt, L. Nicholas, 123, 127
Rotter, Julian B., 56, 73, 132, 148
Russ, F. A., 96, 112

Safilios-Rothschild, Constantina, 110, 112
Satir, Virginia, 149, 150, 169-171, 172
Satisficing rule, 96-97
Satislex rule, 96-97
Sawer, Barbara J., 110, 112
Scanzoni, John, 137, 148
Scheck, Dennis C., 73
Schroder, Harold M., 41, 52, 115, 117, 118, 127
Sears, Paul B., 184, 185
Shannon, William V., 65, 73
Shepard, Paul, 184, 185
Simon, Herbert A., 96, 98, 99, 112
Slater, Kenneth, 33
Smith, Manual J., 162, 172
Social effects, 47-48, 76-78, 100-105
Spencer, Robert F., 72
Standards, 77, 87, 133-136, 145
Starr, Martin K., 123, 127
Strategies for choice, 122-126
Streufert, Siegfried, 41, 52
Strodtbeck, Fred L., 69, 72
Suedfeld, Peter, 117, 127

Sussman, M. B., 80-81, 89

Tactical decision, 107
Tallman, Irving, 39-40, 42, 52
Tasker, Grace, 145, 148
Technical decisions, 100, 105
Technology, 6, 16, 18, 19, 28, 29, 30, 36-39, 46, 69
Thompson, P., 148
Time, 70, 94-95, 120, 129
Toffler, Alvin, 116, 127
Turil, E., 72
Turner, Ralph H., 77, 89, 110, 112, 157, 160-161, 172

Uncertainty, 113-127

Values, 6, 7, 8, 54, 58, 63-72, 129-131, 133, 142
Vickers, Sir Geoffrey, 12, 14, 135, 148

Waring, Ethel B., 142-143, 148
Weick, Karl, 131, 148
Wetters, Doris E., 137, 148
White House Conference, 75
Withey, Stephen, 183, 184
Witkin, H., 55, 73
Wolfe, D. M., 110, 111
Wyden, Peter, 151, 162-163, 171

Yablonsky, Lewis, 49, 52